1-28/10

SLAVERY AND CHRISTIANITY THE UNTOLD STORY

To
My Bobby,
You are my brother and
my friend. I pray for
your gift with songs.
I pray that my book will
encourage you to go home
to Africa.

By

Marlene L. Garland-Hill

Love,
Rev. Dr. Marlene L. Garland Hill
Nana /Afi'a

ISBN: 978-1-61529-006-2

Published by:

Vision Publishing

1115 D Street

Ramona, CA 92065

www.visionpublishingservices.com

1-800-9-VISION

Acknowledgement Page

First, I thank God for choosing me to be his servant. I also thank Him for intrusting me with the title, "Slavery and Christianity the Untold Story" for my dissertation. What an honor it is to receive an assignment to complete this research project at such a time in history as this. "To God be the Glory"!

I owe a debt of thanks and gratitude to my husband Bill for his love, patience, support, faith, and financial sacrifice. I also thank him for traveling with me when time permitted and for his understanding and encouragement during my journeys alone.

This dissertation is dedicated in memory of my parents Sylvester and Patricia Gary. I thank them for their love. I also thank them for insulating me with a strong belief in God, and in knowing that all things are possible through Christ who strengthens me.

To my son Charles Garland, thank you for your constant encouragement, support, and spiritual commitment to God. Thank you immensely for creating the front and back cover and producing music for me to use with this important project.

Thank you Daniel Adjai, my tour consultant and guide during two of my visits to Ghana. May God bless you for prophetically telling me that the truth must be told about what took place in the Slave Castles and Forts of Ghana.

Foreword

Dr. Marlene L. Garland-Hill has gifted society with a rich historical study of slavery, undergirded by Christianity and other religions in Africa, Europe, the British Aisles and the West Indies. Slavery is the unconscionable sin of the dehumanization of human beings by other human beings in the name of the same God who made, saved, blessed and dignified all human beings. Slavery is a system instigated by people in order to deny all slaves of their right to be, will to be and power to be. When any persons lose their freedom they lose their humanity. To be human, according to the 18th century Enlightenment philosopher Immanuel Kant, is to be an end in oneself, and not just a means to the ends and aims of others. Slavery takes a mother and makes her a baby-machine. Slavery takes a man and turns him into a stud for the purpose of breeding, but that man is not permitted to assume the responsibility and opportunity of parenting and guiding that child to maturity.

The presupposition of slavery is that the enslaved do not deserve to be free because they are inferior to persons of other races, economic groups, social classes and religious groups. That is strictly an unbiblical notion. It is a violation of Catholic principles, Orthodox beliefs, Jewish social ethics and Protestant values of humanity, liberty and equality. The Bible that is embraced and affirmed by several religions states at the out-set that all humankind is made in the image and likeness of God. That statement leaves no room for any prejudice, assumption or beliefs that restrict the divine or ultimate content that resides in all people, all races, all nations, all social classes and all religions. This statement found in Genesis includes all people and denies no people, restricts no race, excludes no social, academic or economic class. We are not human because we are white, or yellow, or red, or black. We are all human and we each have divine value and ultimate acceptance. God made us and called us into personal relationship and creative partnership with God:

"So God created humankind in his image, in the image of God he created them, male and female he created them. God blessed them and said to them, "Be fruitful and multiply, and fill the earth and subdue it; and have dominion over the fish of the sea and over the birds of the air and over every living thing that moves upon the earth." Genesis 1:27, 28.

We notice that God gives human beings dominion not over other human beings but over fish, fowl and lower animals <u>only</u>.

There are some Jewish, Christian and Muslim thinkers who extend man's humanity to humans beyond humans to the religious ethical mandate to purify the entire cosmos, detoxify the lakes, rivers and oceans, and even show kindness to the other animals of the earth in the practice of what Albert Schweitzer called, "the universally mandated reverence for life." All life is sacred. All humans are holy. All souls are precious, and all religions are accountable to this crucial mandate:

"You shall love the Lord your God with all your heart, and with all your soul, and with all your mind. This is the greatest and fist commandment. And the second is like it: You shall love your neighbor as yourself." On these two commandments hang all the law and the prophets." Matthew 22: 37-40.

Rather than applying these divine laws to everyone, Christianity and all other religions have been guilty of dehumanizing excluded groups of human beings who are deemed by human standards to be inferior or inherently subordinate to those who make themselves superior and holier to those who differ or disagree with their limited understandings of reality and their exclusivistically narrowed interpretations of the scriptures. Narrow, exclusive literal interpretations of Holy Scriptures are sinful distortions of what is affirming and universal into ideologies and restricted covenants of exclusion, rejection, enslavement and exploitation.

They quote the few passages of scripture where slavery is approved and governed, while they miss the grand and glorious passages in the Bible that unifies and affirms "all creatures of our God and King."

It isn't enough just to quote passages of scripture out-of-context; but to understand each single unit of scripture in their specific, historical, linguistic and theological context. The fact is that slavery in Israel, in Christianity and in ancient Islam did not express itself as perpetual, inter-generational and permanent exploitation and incarceration. The slave had a limited term in Israel and in the Ancient New East. During one's enslavement in Biblical societies, the slaves could marry the children of their masters and enter into the free society of the well-to-do. Abraham had a son by an Egyptian slave woman, Hagar, and that child was not a slave, but a prince whom God blessed and endowed as God had exalted and enriched Isaac, son of Abraham by Sarah, his wife. Moreover, Jacob had sons by his female slaves and they were all entitled to perpetual freedom and wealth. Slavery had ethical, theological and beneficial limits in Biblical times. It also was limited by time, and in the year of Jubilee all slaves were conscientiously liberated to join their human and religious societies as dignified equals and not depraved inferiors.

Jesus never endorsed slavery; but Jesus took sides, not with the oppressors of human beings, but with the liberators of all people. He said in the inauguration of his ministry:

"The Spirit of the Lord is upon me, because he has anointed me to preach good news to the poor, He hath sent me to proclaim release to the captives and recovery of sight to the blind, to let the oppressed go free, to proclaim the year of the Lord's favor. (That's Jubilee freedom and justice for all). Luke 4:14-19

We are grateful to Dr. Marlene Garland-Hill for showing the unconscionable failure of all religions to practice these salient theological and ethical principles so plain in all the scriptures of all the religions. It is a shame before God that Christians, Muslims and Jews in the 15th century A.D. chose to create and practice the permanent, self-perpetuating, inter-generational slavery which Africans were forced to suffer. Dr. Marlene Garland-Hill has stated her case and proven her hypotheses through detailed travel itineraries and primary historical documents. This book is packed. I urge you to unpack it for the enlightenment of the head and the redemption of the soul. By this book, human life on earth will be enhanced as it becomes more humane. Remember Jewish philosopher Martin Buber said, "One cannot 'thingify' another human being without 'thingifying' himself and herself in the premise and in the process." Dr. Garland-Hill's book helps us to 'de-thingify' the human community and purify the natural cosmos.

Charles G. Adams,
Pastor, Hartford Memorial Baptist Church, Detroit, Michigan
Professor, Harvard Divinity School, Cambridge, Massachusetts

TABLE OF CONTENTS

CHAPTER I – INTRODUCTION

CHAPTER II – REVIEW OF THE LITERATURE

CHAPTER III – RESEARCH

PART VII– RECOMMENDATIONS FOR ADDITIONAL
RESEARCH

CHAPTER I – INTRODUCTION

The Trans-Atlantic Slave Trade

This dissertation was preordained to articulate the cruelty and residual effects of the Trans-Atlantic Slave trade. The Slave trade was such a fundamental part of history, that it deserved a pilgrimage to Africa and Europe in search of the truth for this dissertation. At the height of the Slave trade, at least 80 Slave castles and forts also referred to as Slave dungeons existed along the West Coast of Africa. Approximately 30 of the structures and commemorative landmarks remain today. Goree Island off the coast of Senegal was the last stop for many of the enslaved Africans shipped to the Americas from West Africa. Most of the Slave castles and forts are currently museums sites. Unfortunately, some of them have been painted and or whitewashed to cover or present more humanizing portrayals of what really took place for hundreds of years in those horrid places.

The majority of the information circulated in America on the subject of the Slave trade in text books and other literature focuses on the disparaging history of the enslaved Africans who survived the middle passage and after they reached the Americas, Europe, the West Indies, and the Caribbean. Not as much attention has been directed towards the enslaved Africans' experiences prior to them leaving Africa on Slave ships. The involvement of Christians and Christianity in the Slave trade was not disclosed to any great degree. The lack of awareness by many African Americans and others in reference to the role of Christians and Christianity in the Slave trade, the pre-middle passage, and middle passage history of enslaved Africans justifies the necessity for this dissertation.

One of the goals of this dissertation is to bear witness and add credence to the Trans-Atlantic Slave trade history. Think of the worst criminal and sexual crimes that could possibly be perpetrated against a human being. Now triple that thought and you still may not come close to imagining or comprehending the heinous, despicable, unconscionable brutality, and chastisement suffered by Africans at the hands of Slave captures, traders, and owners. Greed, control, religion, fear, hatred, racism, and a loathing for a particular race of people funded and fueled the Trans-Atlantic Slave trade.

"Textbooks in the United States have perpetuated the notion of an early role of the Dutch in the Atlantic slave trade by citing a passage from captain John Smith's old history of Virginia, which includes the following reference to the first African slaves arriving in the North American mainland. "About the last of August (1619) came a Dutch man of Warre that sold us twenty negars." A closer examination of the circumstances confirms that the ship plundering expedition against the Spanish in the West Indies it had captured at or in the vicinity of the Jamestown settlement. The identity of the particular Dutch ship has unfortunately never been established."[1] (Postma 12)

Christians and Christianity were accused of being major contributors in the enslavement of the African people. The role Christians and Christianity played in the Trans-Atlantic Slave trade has been 'swept under the rug' so to speak. This theory will be unearthed to prove or disprove responsibility. New Christians like Diego Caballero were easily enticed by the prominence and monetary gains of the Slave trade.

"The slave merchants of Seville also included New Christians, as was the case in Lisbon. For example prominent in the 1540s was Diego Caballero, a converso from Sanlucar, who began to make his fortune in Hispaniola in 1510 or so and much increased it when he went to Seville." [2] (Thomas 128)

Graphic descriptions, literature, and pictures recounting the atrocities surrounding the Slave castles, forts, dungeons, Slave rivers, Slave caves, mass graves, middle passage, and the use of the Bible and Christianity to benefit the Slave trade are portrayed in subsequent chapters. This dissertation is a daunting task because Slavery and Christianity are very sensitive subjects.

"While there is a valid argument for choosing 1444, historians have generally agreed upon the year 1441 as that in which the modern slave trade was, so to speak, officially declared open. In that year ten Africans from the northern Guinea Coast were shipped to Portugal as a gift to Prince Henry the Navigator. Obtained as ransom for other, superior 'moors' who had been kidnapped after being hunted down like wild animals by the Portuguese sailors, these ten Africans were brought back in triumph by a modest trading expedition commanded by a young prote'ge' of Prince Henry named Antam Gonclvez. They had not, however, been captured for sale, but simply to be shown to Prince Henry in the same way that rare plants, exotic butterflies or tropical birds might have been shown."[3] (Hennessy 8)

The Slave Trade Foretold

Many historical events are foretold of in the Bible. The Trans-Atlantic Slave trade was no different. Deuteronomy 28:68 mentions the African Hebrews being returned to Egypt again, this time by way of ships and sold as bondsmen and bondswomen. *"there they would be sold unto their enemies for bondsmen and bondswomen."*[4]

Africans were taken by ships and sold into Slavery. Why were they the people God referred to in scripture?

"The African Hebrew tribes fled into all parts of Africa to escape the tirades and slaughter of Hebrews by Titus that led to the destruction of Jerusalem in 70 A.D. Little did they know that their flight into Africa would change the history of Africa forever. Once Jerusalem was destroyed the remaining inhabitants migrated to the sub Saharan regions of Africa to survive. The survivors were the last of the African Hebrews from Jerusalem. This brought about the final phase of chastisement and the disbursement of the people of Africa into Europe and the lands of the Americas, the New World. The African Slaves were transported to the New World (a second Egypt) in the bottoms of Slaves ships, under the most inhumane conditions. These people were stretched out face-to-face in two lines, and in the space between their feet with others lying on their backs. The ships were packed to the brim."[5] (Felder 334)

Future Intent

The future intent of this dissertation is to encourage cross-cultural and biblical discussions to stimulate the thinking of individuals affected directly or indirectly by the Trans-Atlantic Slave trade. This research project will hopefully bring awareness to some and closure to others longing to re-connect with African heritage and lineage. It may also serve as a future source of information for individuals seeking answers to journeys, treatment, and conditions enslaved Africans endured prior to leaving Africa and on Slave ships. People of color have the same dream that Dr. Martin Luther King, Jr. had for his four children, which was, "to be judged by the content of their character, and not by the color of their skin."[6](King)

Endnotes:

(1) The Dutch in the Atlantic Slave Trade 1600-1815- Johannes Menne Postma - Cambridge University Press 1990 - (Page 12)

(2) The History of The Trans Atlantic Slave Trade by Hugh Thomas 1440-1870 1997 Simon & Schuster Inc. New York New York (Page 128)

(3) The Atlantic Slave Traders 1441-1807 James Pope-Hennessy - Castle Books - 1967 – (Page 8)

(4) Deut. 28:68

(5) *Holy Bible King James Version* - Cain Hope Felder - James C. Winston Publishing. 1993 – (Page 334)

(6) I Have A Dream - Dr. Martin Luther King, Jr . Washington, DC - August 28, 1963

CHAPTER II – REVIEW OF THE LITERATURE

Vision for God's Purpose

The inspiration for this dissertation was initiated by a vision from God. While enrolled in a Masters in Ministry class on healing at the Assemblies of God Seminary in Lakeland Florida, the professor asked for volunteers to be prayed for. The purpose of the class was to prepare students for setting up different types of prayer ministries outside the confines of the church. As a volunteer, the professor picked the members of my prayer team. While grateful for the first team's prayers, I was moved to ask permission to pick the prayer team. The professor honored my request. A Pastor originally from Ghana took the lead in praying. He placed his hands on my shoulders along with the rest of the prayer team. The team was praying in the spirit, when suddenly I saw a vision of me on a ship crossing an ocean to what looked like Africa, except I had never been to Africa. Then chains broke. Tears began steaming down my face, because I did not know what it meant. By the time the prayer teams stopped praying, the entire class was weeping. The professor asked what happened, and I shared the vision with the class. Our entire class began weeping again.

While reading the Bible that evening Numbers 1:18 and a commentary detailing the importance of lineage stood out.

"And they assembled the entire congregation together on the first day the second month, and they declared their pedigrees after their families, by the house of their fathers, according to the number of the names, from twenty years old and upward. by their polls." [7] *(Num. 1:18)*

The commentary read, "The Declaration of Lineage-At various points in history, the African Hebrews have had to declare their pedigrees (lineages). The same holds true throughout Africa, where declaring their family line is part of traditional education for children in many African societies. The genealogy gives a sense of depth, historical belongingness, a feeling of deep-rootedness and a sense of sacred obligation to extend the genealogical line. Slave owners made certain that the nicknames given to the Slaves disconnected them from the African land, language, and culture, thus taking away one of the basic steps to racial and cultural pride."[8] (Felder 210)

The Holy Spirit revealed through scripture that you need to know where you came from before you will know where you are going! That was an epiphany, because for the next few years, practically every part of my life relating to Africa pointed to Ghana. Food, clothing, people, art, music, and the languages associated with Ghana were constantly placed in my path. Three years later, God revealed prophetically in November that I would be visiting Ghana the following February. This happened on a Thursday, and by Sunday, there was a confirmation.

Prophecy Revealed

Two opportunities to visit Africa came about in the same week in November. One was to visit the Gambia and Senegal with a group from Hartford Memorial Baptist Church. The other was a trade mission to Ghana for business. I chose to visit Africa with our Church. Choosing God's purpose resulted in Ghana being added to our trip by surprise at the last moment. We left for Africa in February! The intended purpose for God's vision on the ship was revealed during the journey to Africa. The journey began with a visit to the Gambia and Senegal. When our church group arrived in The Gambia, it was as if we literally stepped back in time. The majority of the African people wore traditional African attire. There were ox drawn carts competing for the right of way in traffic with cars, trucks, and buses. The other significant factor was that this journey was arranged by God to begin during Lent, so a fast was observed by Dr. Pierson and me immediately. We visited a village and school that our church supports in the Gambia, and the Slave castle on Goree Island off the coast of Senegal. The vision from class resurfaced when our group stood in front of a statue of a freed African man and woman holding broken chains outside the

Slave castle on Goree Island.

Gambian brother Cherno, Alberta, our tour guide Abduli, and Marlene in Front of the Freedom Statue on Goree Island

We toured the men, women, and children's dungeons in the Slave castle. The foul stench of the past was still present. Standing in the door of no return that once lead to Slave ships, took my husband Bill and my breath and strength away. We both had a weird feeling, as if the presence of the African Ancestors was with us. Our next stop was Albreda/Juffureh, the ancestral home of Alex Haley, the "author of "Roots". This was the coastal village that Kunta Kinte in the movie "Roots" was kidnapped from during the Slave trade. Our group spoke to and took pictures with Benta, the eldest living relative of the Kinte family and other family members in the village. Benta would not reveal her age. Unfortunately our group was informed that Benta passed away a few months after we returned to the US.

(Left Albreda: Right: Juffureh Benta Bottom: Benta, Marlene, and Bill)

Our next stop was Ghana a few days later. We toured Elmina Slave Castle on the Cape Coast of Ghana. The treatment Africans received at that Slave castle was just as appalling, as or worse than on Goree Island. We listened to more stories about the rapes torture, beatings, and killings of Africans daily. Our group cried some more for the African Ancestors. But, at Elmina castle, touring the chapel inside the castle, and listening to the details of the brutal rapes of women and girls was too much for us to handle. We toured the rest of the Slave Castle in anger. While visiting the book store, I blurted out, "I know God brought me here." The Holy Spirit just revealed it to me. "Slavery and Christianity, the Untold Story is the title of my dissertation." Our tour guide Daniel responded, "You have to tell the story of what happened here. The truth must be told."[9] (Adjai)

In Isaiah 6:8, Isaiah heard the voice of the Lord. God asked Isaiah an important question. *"Also I heard the voice of the Lord, saying. Whom shall I send and who will go for us? Then said I, Here am I; send me."*[10] (Isaiah 6:8)

God asked who will go out to speak to this people on His behalf. Isaiah answered the call. Who will speak on behalf of enslaved African men, women, and children beaten, murdered, raped, tortured and maimed on the roads of Africa, in the Slave castles and forts, and on the Slave ships? Who will speak on behalf of the Africans thrown to their deaths as their skeletons lay at the bottom of oceans and seas? The descendants of African Ancestors sold and traded as human cargo deserve to have all of their history revealed and preserved. Your humble servant asks you to send her.

Hundreds of Years of Tears

There is an assumption that most people have heard of the Trans-Atlantic Slave trade or know what a Slave castle or fort is. People of diverse nationalities and backgrounds were asked what they knew about the Slave trade, Slave castles, forts, rivers, caves, or mass graves in Africa for this dissertation. Some knew or heard of the Slave trade, but a disturbing number of about 90% of people questioned admitted that they never heard of a Slave castle, or any of the other above mentioned Slave sites. Over one hundred years have passed since the abolishment of Slavery, and there is still uneasiness when discussing the Slave trade. The chains of silence linking Christians and Christianity to the Trans-Atlantic Slave trade needs to be broken. The African people were taken against their will from villages and homes. This wrong should not be simply part of the past when it is still affecting the present and the future of enslaved African descendants.

Physical or mental Slavery holds a person or people captive for the captures own purpose, profit, or gratification against the captives will. One person takes ownership over another. The captives are normally mistreated, brainwashed, and intimidated by their captures. They are usually taken by force, traded, given, or sold to someone else. One controls and the other is controlled. There were no human, civil, or any other rights for the enslaved Africans during the Trans-Atlantic Slave trade.

Do we place stumbling blocks in our brothers and sisters way when we are in positions of authority? We are all centers of influence in thoughts, deeds, and words that flow from our hearts to our lips. People should be careful of their thoughts and spoken words, because opinions of influential people enslaved the continent of Africa for almost four hundred years. We are all children of God, and deserve to be treated as such.

"Slavery is sometimes regarded as a tragic anomaly of history-a dark cloud, threatening but small, on the receding horizon of the past. But it was no anomaly, and its legacies are with us still. The form of slavery that sprang up in the Americas was vastly unlike serfdom in medieval Europe or slavery anywhere else in the world. It was a mainspring of early economic development and the source of enormous wealth, in the form of unpaid labor, for white colonists and their political masters in Europe. The colonizing powers recognized almost from the beginning that African slaves were the only possible remedy for the labor shortages that plagued their New World dominions; slaves mined the precious metals and harvested the sugar, indigo and to bacco that made colonization worthwhile." [11] (Morganthau)

By the time the Slaves reached the coast of Ghana, they had already traveled in some cases hundreds of miles from other neighboring countries and further inland.

The Trans-Atlantic Slave trade is a subject that people would prefer to bury as part of the past. It is not easy for anyone to acknowledge, accept, or thrash out, because of the pain and injustice associated with its' horrific and sweltering history. Is it because people can't accept the truth? The very mention of the Trans-Atlantic Slave trade invokes a multiplicity of feelings; hurt, anger, trepidation, resistance, disgust, and guilt just to name a few. The Africans suffered humiliation, torment, sorrow, indignation, disrespect, inequality, and were stripped of their heritage and culture. Like an earthquake, the aftershocks continuously resonate throughout the world. Racial discrimination, segregation, and inequality are devastating residuals of the Slave trade. Most African American ancestral roots lead to West Africa.

When the Slave trade is mentioned by African descendants, they are encouraged to "get over it." This request is not only insensitive, but disrespectful to the Ancestors who suffered and lost their lives because of it. Absent from the body, the ancestors are present with the Lord. The past can not be erased, but we can remember the courage and sacrifice of millions of African lives. We can make sure that the Ancestors suffering was not in vain by removing hate from our hearts and actions towards others whom we deem to be different from us. God commands you to love even your enemies. After people tour the Slave castles, forts, and other slave sites that is probably one of the hardest requests to embrace.

Documented personal accounts from some of the captives are important to this project. Only God can heal the open wounds of Slavery. No one can free you but God. Let us look at what historians and other authors left out of the history books and other literature regarding the Slave dungeons, castles, forts, Christians, and Christianity before during and immediately following the middle passage. Could the stereotypical description of the African people by the Catholic Church have played a significant role in the

Slave trade? The scriptures used by cunning Christians, Slave traders, missionaries, and captures to justify the Slave trade will be explored in this dissertation.

The African ancestors are worthy of having their suffering acknowledged, not silenced, dismissed, or forgotten. The Atlantic Slave trade should never simply be explained as part of the past, because unfortunately Slavery still exists today. A Ghanaian visiting Elmina castle said the past should be forgotten.

"Those things happened in the old days," said Marian Acquaye, a 29-year-old Ghanaian seamstress who brought a half-dozen nieces and nephews to visit Cape Coast. "I think we should forget all that and be together, united as friends."[12] (Brown)

Europeans forced Africans to build castles, forts, and dungeons in Africa and other countries that held them captive. Many enslaved African descendants desire to re-connect the broken chains of lost family lineage and remove the shackles of racism, injustice, and inequality that continue to plague people of color around the world. *Then the LORD said unto Cain, Where is your brother Abel? "He said, I do not know; am I my brother's keeper? And the Lord said, What have you done? Listen; your brother's blood is crying out to me from the ground!"* [13] *(Gen. 4:9-10)*

The voices and the blood of enslaved Africans cry out from their graves. Bloodstains are still visible on the walls and floors of dungeons in some of the Slave castles and forts. The stench of feces and death can not be white washed or painted over.

"Uncovering the whole truth about slavery is a difficult task for scholars even today. The slaves themselves left relatively few accounts of their lives in captivity, and slaveholders tended for obvious reasons to be reticent about the realities of the system they controlled. The conditions of slavery varied dramatically from place to place and from century to century: depending on circumstances and the attitudes of white colonials, the treatment of slaves ranged from relatively benign paternalism to almost unimaginable brutality."[14](Morganthau)

One of the first steps in moving beyond the pain of Slavery is to unveil the truth about the Slave traders, owners, and captures of Africans. It was a Slave raid instead of the Slave trade. European countries fought each other over who would own the right to enslave Africans. Africans were kidnapped, hunted, brutalized, beat, branded, shackled, chained, raped, burned, murdered, degraded, demoralized, and dehumanized. Slave traders kidnapped, traded, bought, and sold precious human beings for profit and treated them worse than animals. How will individuals know they are enslaved unless they understand what Slavery entails? One of the most important reasons for characterizing the contemptuous plots, devices, and tactics the Europeans and others used to enslave people is to avert the reoccurrence of the Trans-Atlantic Slave trade.

The majority of the human cargo shipped during the middle passage to Europe, North and South America, the Caribbean, and other continents passed through "doors of no return" in Ghana, Senegal, The Gambia, Nigeria, Angola, Sierra Leone and other African countries. Many Africans jumped to their deaths at the doors of no return in Slave castles and forts to avoid boarding the Slave ships to points unknown. Thousands of Africans are buried beneath the deep waters of seas and oceans and in the jungles and rivers of Africa. When Slavers thought they would be caught for kidnapping Africans after it became illegal, the Slavers threw the Africans overboard to get rid of the evidence.

"Doors of No Return in Ghana"

Enslaved Africans were branded with a hot iron on their chest, back, or arm right before they were forced onto Slave ships. Many of the captives died from the pain, or passed out because the pain was so excruciating, or because they had not been given any food. Some of them endured long walks through the tunnels of castles and forts to the Slave ships with heavy shackles around their necks and feet attached one to another. In one Slave castle, the door of no return was also used by Slave captures to kidnap unsuspecting workers and children. The families were persuaded to bring their children and other family members to the Slave castles and forts to work in exchange for traded items. The captures would force the Africans through the door of no return that was too high off the ground to climb back up into the castle. The Europeans have the audacity to have a cross marking the spot where the Slave ships were waiting. European countries fought one another over who would own the right to enslave the African people!

"Ghana has shown a substantial African involvement in the trade. Typically, after an inter-tribal war, the prisoners taken by the winning side were sold to the castles. Then there were traders arriving at the Gold Coast from the north with slaves. Individuals also kidnapped people to sell them into slavery. Dr Perbi's research has revealed that some African traders supplied as many as 15,000 slaves per year to European merchants. Several African-Americans who have decided to settle in their ancestral continent live near the castles and take an active interest in their preservation. When tourist authorities opened cafes and bars inside the castles and started to clean and whitewash the dungeons, African-Americans staged a sit-in in protest at what they saw as a desecration of a shrine to the tragic crime of slavery. The authorities backed down: the cafes were moved and the paint pots put away." [15] (History Today)

What was done to the African people was not private, because God saw it all. Full responsibility for Slavery must be acknowledged to move forward and for healing to begin. Once the responsibility is acknowledged, then what? Denying the Slave trade will not erase it. It is possible to set people free in our minds and in our hearts. If more people would do that, racism would disappear.

The Trans-Atlantic Slave trade started with the Portuguese. The Dutch and English participation was not far behind. Profits and colonialism continuously fueled the Slave trade. Only God can heal the open wounds of slavery. The Slave castles and forts of Africa date back to the 14th century. They were commissioned by different European countries and used African labor to build them.

"Most of the captives of 1444 had been taken by the Portuguese in a village where '... they [the Portuguese], shouting out, "St James, St George, and Portugal," at once attacked them, killing and taking all they could. Then might you see mothers forsaking their children, and husbands their wives, each striving to escape as best they could. Some drowned themselves in the water, others thought to escape by hiding under their huts, others stowed their children among the seaweed, where our men found them afterwards...'" [16] (Thomas 1)

King Henry the Navigator of Portugal and Roman Catholic bishops participated fully in the kidnappings of Africans to enslave them.

"The kidnappings brought a lot of money to the Portuguese king, Henry the Navigator, his captains and the other promoters of the expeditions, including the bishops of the Roman Catholic Church. In 1442, Pope Eugenious IV made it all official by approving King Henry's slave expeditions to Africa in the papal bull, *Illius Qui*. "Then, in the 1450s, Popes Nicholas V and Calixtus III gave an even warmer approval for the (slave) undertakings in three further bulls," writes Hugh Thomas." (Adibe and Boateng 24)[17]

The Veil of Truth Unfolding

Imagine a church built on the top floor of Slave castles and forts with the female dungeons located on the same floor or directly beneath the church. At Elmina Slave Castle and other sites, male Slave traders worshipped God in their churches in the Slave castles or on the grounds of the castle and forts. The female Slaves, which also included girls between the ages of 8 to 16 years were brought to the bedrooms of the captains and other men and brutally raped over and over again by one or more Slave traders simultaneously. These rapes occurred the entire time these women and children were in the dungeons over one to three months or until the next Slave ships arrived. This type of abuse and other accounts of torture, kidnappings, murders, and hell on earth experiences went on for months. The abuse did not end when they left on the Slave ships. Strong Africans survived the abuse and torture in the Slave castles and during the middle passage only to experience more of the same from Slave owners that purchased and sold them numerous times.

"The rape of African women is well established in the literature throughout the Americas; it was necessarily violent in nature. Untold numbers of girls and women were made to endure the violation, sometimes repeatedly, and that fact alone may help explain the incidence of abortion and infanticide."[18] (Gomez 122)

The African women who refused the advances of the Slave masters who raped them repeatedly resulted in their deaths in many instances. When some of women refused the advances of the captures, they were raped anyway or forced to stand in the middle of the Slave castle courtyard with a cannon ball in each hand and their arms outstretched high in the air for long hours in the hot sun to punish them. These women were used as examples for other captives to show them what would happen if they refused to go along with the rapes. Women, girls, and yes men, and boys were raped and or tortured, and or murdered for refusing the abuse. Some Africans committed suicide. They knew that by ending their lives they would escape the torturous lives that lie before them. It is believed that only one third of the captives survived the middle passage and the abuse at the Slave castles and forts and torture by the Slave owners that purchased them.

A person never knows how far one will go, especially when they have lost everything and in particularly their dignity. That is when death may have seemed like a better option than enslavement. Enslaved Africans lost their families. Some men saw their wives, daughters, and sons raped in front of them, and their villages burned. Their dignity was stripped away from them at the Slave rivers which were renamed the last bath. The Slave traders and captures washed the Africans' bodies; the men and the women. The humiliation and shame the Africans must have felt.

"One resisted not only the physical status of slavery but also the devaluation of the African person, which is about culture in the final analysis. As it became impossible to separate slavery from the African, so the fight against slavery and the insistence on African cultural forms became one and the same struggle for many-but of course, not for all. [19] (Gomez 127)

The Church Condones Slavery

No one from Europe, the Americas, or the Christian Church, stepped in to stop the Trans-Atlantic Slave trade when it first began. Nearly four hundred years of terror reined over the continent of Africa. Prior to the Trans-Atlantic Slave Trade, Slavery was used for the repayment of debts in the form of indentured servitude. Warped theology supported the use of the Bible, prayer, and Christianity to enslave the African people.

"God's prophecy upon Israel to "bring them into Egypt again with ships" was fulfilled. Over 100 million people were either taken as captives or killed in the Slave wars. About one-third of the Africans taken from their homes died on the way to the coast of Africa, and at the Slave castles, and another third died at sea, so only one third actually survived to become laborers in the New Word."[20] (Felder 334)

Things are not always as they seem. Slave traders and Christians used the Bible and Christianity to deceive the kings and chiefs in Africa into trading and selling their people into Slavery. Ironically, the Bible and Christianity were also used to some degree in freeing the enslaved Africans. Why did churches in Europe and the Americas condone the mistreatment and profits gained from the Slave trade? Did some of them own Slaves directly? Did God instruct the Catholic Popes and other Christians to enslave Africans?

"The Anglican Society for the Propagation of the Gospel in Foreign Parts owned many slaves in the Caribbean – in fact the word 'SOCIETY' was branded on their chests with a red-hot iron to identify them as property of the SPG. For most Britons the brutality of the slave trade was out of sight, out of mind. British slave-traders were carrying almost 40,000 slaves from Africa to the New World every single year, yet there was no public outcry." [21] (Coffey 2006)

The Bible was misused, laws were promulgated, lies were told, and opinions were formed that permanently affected Africa and its people. Africans were robbed of their heritage, dignity, and human rights. Enslaved Africans entered the pits of hell as captives of the Slave trade. Lost forever were land, assets, families, names, royal inheritance, and family lineage. Africa was a continent of people who traditionally opened their boarders to trade and shared their possessions and land with others. Stereotypical images, information, and interpretations of enslaved Africans portrayed and communicated through story telling, in history books, and other documentation in regards to the Trans-Atlantic slave trade requires an awakening.

The Thirteenth Amendment of the Declaration of Independence declared Slavery invalid in America hundreds of years after it began. It took a civil war to end Slavery officially in America. This country was supposedly the land of the free, for everyone except Africans and Native Americans. What was the middle passage? "Having been purchased on the African coast, the slaves destined for America would cross the Atlantic in a journey that became know as the "Middle Passage." The manner in which these slaves were carried and the mortality they suffered have been one of the most notorious issues in the study of the Atlantic slave trade. A popular literature has painted this part of the slave experience as uniquely evil and intently more inhuman than any other of the horrors of the slave life." [22] (Klein 130)

God, where are you? Why is this happening to us? Captive after captive probably asked similar questions. Slavery was not good in any form or fashion, and there is no way to justify that wrong. No one feared God in the days of the Trans-Atlantic Slave trade. If they did, the Slave trade wouldn't have lasted as long as it did. There have been devastating results from Slavery. Eyes can be deceiving, but the heart is what counts. Man's ways are not God's ways. For most people survival is about self and selfishness of the fittest. Jesus came to earth in human flesh, and man still would not listen. God instructed man to feed his sheep, not steal his sheep. He said take care of the widows and orphans not sell them!

"Both Christianity and Islam asserted the unique value of the individual human being, as created by God for his special purposes. Yet, for their own special purposes, Christian and Muslim societies long sanctioned the capture, sale, ownership, and use of men, women and children from black Africa. We can never know the extent of the human cost. It is certain that many millions lost their lives in the warfare and raiding that provided the captives for slavery. Millions more died in the process of collection, initial transport, and storage. "[23] (Segal 1)

Stories have been told for years by enslaved African descendants that the first Europeans were carrying Bibles when they first arrived in Ghana. Europeans supposedly came in peace on behalf of the Governments or Monarchies they represented. Death and enslavement warrants for four hundred years into the future were signed when Africans traded people for goods. As the Europeans greed grew, kidnappings beatings, torturing, and killings increased for individuals who tried to escape. Entire villages were burned to make sure that if any Africans did escape, there would be no home for them to return to. "British slave trading had begun in the late sixteenth century, and grew apace during the seventeenth and eighteenth centuries. By 1807, around three million slaves had been transported to the Americas on British ships. The trade was occasionally denounced by Christians. Richard Baxter declared that slave-traders were 'fitter to be called devils than Christians', and the Puritan Samuel Sewall published America's first antislavery tract, *The Selling of Joseph* (1700). But most Christians in the early eighteenth century accepted slavery as a fact of life. The evangelist George Whitefield deplored the cruelty of slave-owners in the American South, but did not condemn slavery itself – indeed, he owned over fifty slaves in Georgia." [24] (Coffey 2006)

The Bible provided the parameters for the use of Slavery. In the Bible, the captives were freed after six years. .

"And if thy brother, a Hebrew man, or a Hebrew woman, be sold unto thee; and serve thee six years; then in the seventh year thou shalt let him go free from thee. And when thou sendest him out free from thee, thou shalt not let him go away empty: Thou shalt furnish him liberally out of thy flock, and out of thy floor, and out of thy winepress: of that wherewith the LORD thy God hath blessed thee thou shalt give unto him. And thou shalt remember that thou wast a bondman in the land of Egypt and the LORD thy God redeemed thee: therefore I command thee this thing to day" [25] (Deut. 15:12-15) The Trans-Atlantic-Slave trade was against God's will based on the Bibles' instructions. The Europeans, Americans, Spaniards, Danes, Swedes, French,

Germans, and others from countries involved in the Slave trade were not justified. Enslaved Africans were not released in the seventh year.

For some strange reason Europeans and Americans thought Africans had no concept of God before they arrived in Africa. Did they forget that Joseph escaped into Africa to save the life of Jesus? Because the Africans did not worship God the way they did, Africans were considered heathens.

"The concept of a Trinity was not shocking or beyond consideration nor was the idea of an indwelling Holy Sprit. However, the stiff, placid liturgical styles of the various churches were altered substantially to accommodate the full expression of the Holy Ghost, within which the dance and ceremony were in every way consistent with African notions of spirit possession. The ring shout, featuring worshipers moving counter clockwise in an ever-quickening circle, was a derivative of West Central African and West African practice and was widespread in North America. In these and other ways, Christianity itself was first converted, facilitating the subsequent conversion of the African to its main tenets. [26] (Gomez 126)

Responsibility or Blame, What Does it Mean?

Europeans and Slave traders stole the African land and natural resources along with the people. Where is the justification for any of this wrong? The blood, sweat, tears, torture, and humiliation of enslaved Africans were used to build the wealth and infrastructure of many countries throughout the world. Slave traders and others used the Bible and Christianity to take what did not lawfully or morally belong to them.

No one can pluck individuals out of God's hands, dead or alive. The resurrection of Jesus Christ and faith of the promise of His return is the assurance of rest for the souls of the enslaved African Ancestors. God knows what they suffered. His love, mercy, and grace are the only agents to change the hard hearts of faithless generations. "Belief in God" is the only way to true freedom. Jesus said, don't worry about the one that can kill the body, worry about the one that can kill the soul. God loves us. He can take the Slave trade that man used for evil, and turn it into good. Repentance and forgiveness are essential for healing the open wounds and evil of the Trans-Atlantic Slave trade. Rev. Bailey provides a good analogy for the responsibility of Christians and Islam in the Slave trade.

"The Christians were the ones who enslaved the Black man, but Islam is a world-wide brotherhood." You may have heard someone say something like this and wondered if it was true. Many books have been written about the shameful treatment of Slaves by Christians in this country, and true Christians offer no excuse for it. The Christian conscience condemns this atrocity and feels it must face and confess all the brutal facts. So, is the involvement of Christians in Slavery a valid reason for leaving Christianity and becoming a Muslim? Not unless Muslims are innocent in this matter.

The highest volume of the Slave trade was in the trans-Atlantic Slave trade from 1451 to 1867. Fage estimates that there was a total of about 12 million Slaves taken from West Africa to Europe and the Americas by "Christian" traders over those 4 centuries." [27] (Bailey vol. 4)

Some people including enslaved African descendants have tried to place the blame on Africans for selling their own people into Slavery.

"We tend to blame the colonial masters. We don't blame ourselves." But on further thought, Awudi added, "Well, our ancestors really shouldn't have sold human beings for gunpowder and drink." [28] (Brown)

Placing the blame for the Trans-Atlantic Slave trade on African rulers and chiefs is a cover up to shift the blame away from the real offenders of the Slave trade. What ever the case may be, by no means does the involvement of African chiefs and kings compare with the responsibility of Europe and the Americas. Europeans and other Slave traders bought and sold precious human beings for profit and merchandise. The African people were kidnapped, oppressed, hunted, brutalized, beat, tortured, branded, shackled, chained, raped, maimed, burned, murdered, degraded, demoralized, and dehumanized. "In his book "Narrative of a Five Years Expedition against the Revolted Negroes of Surinam", Stedman quotes a white colonist who described the torture-execution of a slave: Not long ago, "this colonist told Stedman, "I saw a black man hang'd alive by the ribs, between which with a knife was first made an incision, and then clinch'd an Iron hook with a chain. In this manner, he kept living three days, hanging with head and feet downwards and catching with his tongue the drops of water, it being the rainy season, that were flowing down his bloated breast, while the vultures were picking in the putrid wound." [29] (Morganthau)

The Bible is God's instruction manual for peace, love, promise, mercy, fairness, justice, truth, and treatment of others. The following scripture meant nothing during the Trans-Atlantic Slave trade.

"But when the Pharisees had heard that he had put the Sadducees to silence, they were gathered together. Then one of them, which was a lawyer, asked him a question, tempting him, and saying, Master, which is the great commandment in the law? Jesus said unto him, Thou shalt love the Lord they God with all they heart, and with all they soul, and with all they mind. This is the first and great commandment. And the second is like unto it, Thou shalt love they neighbor as they self. On these two commandments hang all the laws and the prophets." [30] *(Matt. 22:34-40)*

Africans were condemned to torture and possibly death from the time they were either traded for goods or kidnapped by Slave traders. One cannot help but be angry; but anger will not solve or change what happened. Revelation can keep these types of abuses from resurfacing or ever having a significant place in history again. Who is to blame for the Slave trade? African forefathers were not innocent. Some descendants of African Slave traders were asked to apologize for their part in the Trans-Atlantic Slave trade. "TRADITIONAL rulers in Africa have been asked officially to apologise to Americans of Africa descent for the roles their forefathers played in the slave trade.

"It was barbaric for our forefathers to sell their kinsmen to the whiteman for a pittance, and we must take responsibility for their wrong deeds and officially apoligise." Togbe Dzegblade IV, Chief of Adaklu Kodzobi in the Volta Region, had said.

He said this at a durbar held by the chiefs and people of the area for a visiting group of African-Americans. The durbar was symbolic of forgiveness and reconciliation for the roles played by their ancestors in the slave trade." [31] (Tamakloe and Kodzobi 16)

One of the first mental mind games Slave masters forced on enslaved Africans was to erase there connection to Africa by changing their names to European ones or by giving them nicknames prior to leaving Africa. The captives were normally named after the Slave owners that purchased them.

Daniel 1:6-7 and the commentary immediately following, describes the significance of changing a name.

"Now among these were of the children of Judah, Daniel, Hananiah, Mishael, and Azariah:

Unto whom the prince of the eunuchs gave name: for he gave unto Daniel the name of Belteshazzar; and to Hananiah, of Shadrach; and to Mishel, of Meshach; and to Azariah of Abednego." [32] *(Daniel 1:6-7)*

"In biblical thought a name is not a mere label of identification: It is an expression of the essential nature of its bearer.A man's name reveals his character. When Nebuchadnezzar had Daniel and his brothers' names changed into Babylonian names, it was more than a name change, it was intended to affect a change in character. In African/Edenic societies a name and its meaning are important. Nearly all African names have meaning. Some names describe the personality of an individual, or his character, or some key event in his life. The ancient Hebrews and other African /Edenic tribes have placed the same importance on names. This knowledge of name significance adds to the historical value and culture of a people."[33] (Felder 1254)

The Africans suffered heartache, pain, humiliation,

torment, sorrow, and indignation. They were torched and maimed on the roads of Africa, and in the Slave castles and forts. As powerful as the Asantes were, they could not save their own people from Slavery and Colonialism.

"The transfer of all the business interest of the Dutch to the British jeopardized Asante's trade with the South. Not only did Asante lose her possession on the coast by the take-over of the Dutch investments but was also deprived of her lucrative trade of which the Dutch was her greatest partner. The British Government, threatened by the Asante militarism, adopted a devide and rule policy by which the other tribes were liberated from the hegemony of Asante through wars planned and executed actively by the British agents. This was regarded by Asante as an aggression and therefore did not take kindly to British governance of the country. The unprovoked wars against Asante were considered as abuse of Britain's military power and a ploy to dispossess Asante of her motherland by conquest. Asante's lingering suspicion of Britains' policy of exploitation was therefore heightened by British monopoly of both trade and acquisition of her mineral resources. Ostensibly, Asante's insistences of their rights was considered by Britain as a threat to her determination to rule the Gold Coast. Military action was therefore considered most appropriate to crush Asante once and for all." [34] (Danquah 2-3)

If you evaluate what Africa suffered from the loss of almost two-thirds of its people, land, and natural resources during the Trans-Atlantic Slave trade and colonialism, then Africa was disenfranchised. Slave traders and Europeans stole the African land and natural resources along with the people. European countries warred amongst themselves over African land and people that did not belong to them in the first place. Where is the justification for any of this wrong? The blood, sweat, and tears of enslaved Africans were used to build the wealth and infrastructure of many countries as stated earlier. Slave traders and others used the Bible and Christianity to take what did not belong to them. Rev. Bailey did not believe the Christians or Muslims enslaved the Black man.

"So did Christians or Muslims enslave the Black man? Neither! Sinful, greedy human beings of all religions did. It is our corrupt, sinful humanity that stands condemned for the evils of slavery. Furthermore, the slave masters themselves became slaves, because Sin is the real slave master! Jesus said, "I tell you the truth, everyone who sins is a slave to sin ... if the Son sets you free, you will be free indeed." [35] (John 8:34,36) (Bailey vol. 4)

The world has to move beyond racial and economic divides. The fuel and energy of racism and injustice must be turned into equality for all people. In the end, God will have the last word for the punishment of the individuals who enslaved the African people. God does not overlook or excuse sin. Thankfully there will be no discrimination in heaven. He hates sin because of what it does to the ones He loves. It destroys them. When Jesus sets you free you are free in deed. Someone forgot to tell God's people and nations. We must all strive to be acceptable in the eyes of God. It is accomplished by keeping true to His word. Christians claim to believe in God's word. Then why in this day and time do they continue to persecute their brothers and sisters? There are broods of vipers today. Change begins on the inside.

"The difference between Islam and Christendom in the experience of black diaspora is clear today. Despite the prominent part played by individual Christians, including members of the clergy, in opposing slavery and subsequently racist practices, the established Churches long tended to reflect dominant social attitude, sometimes to the extent of having separate sectors for black and white in their congregations. And while dissenting denominations, such as the Methodist and the Baptist, took a socially less supine position, they were wary of provoking their white adherents too far, and were reluctant to cede white organization control. All this, together with enforced or functioning residential segregation, led blacks to found churches and even sects of their own." [36] (Segal 9-10)

Freedom does not mean one is free from Slavery because of mental conditioning drilled into the psyche of enslaved Africans with the Willie Lynch theory that was passed down through the generations from Slavery to the present to pit one person of color against the other. Unfortunately it still exists today. The theory for example pits the dark skinned Africans against the lighter skinned Africans and visa versa. If you put a lighter skinned black person and a darker skinned person or a white person and a black person together in front of a mirror, and ask them who is superior? What would the answer be? The answer is for you to consider the next time you stand next to a person of a different ethnicity. The African descendants often times are made to feel that they are inferior, while other people may feel that it is their rightful place to be superior. Neither one is correct according to God, who created us all in His image. That person is their brother or sister who deserves and should be entitled to the same rights as the other. It would be nice if that were the opinion throughout the world, but it is not. Until equality becomes universal, research projects similar to this will continue to be of interest to people who want a different world and view people through God's eyes.

"White supremacy bred among those discriminated against an imitative high value on lightness of complexion and a corresponding disparagement of dark features. Yet the very exclusiveness of white supremacy guarded the frontier against all but a few furtive crossings. It was this that essentially promoted and secured the existence of a vast black diaspora, increasing conscious of its peculiar identity, its collective past, and its cultural heritage." [37] (Segal 8)

The Trans-Atlantic Slave trade supposedly ended over one hundred years ago. Yet racism, inequality, and division between people of different races based on the color of one's skin keeps oppression alive and well. More than an apology is compulsory to absolve the African holocaust. The world must be willing to move beyond racial and economic divides. The fuel and energy of racism, injustice, and inequality should be turned into equality for all people. That is a dream or is it?

"Bless your enemy, and you rob him of his ammunition." His arrows will be transmuted into blessings. This law is true of nations as well as individuals. Bless a nation, send love and goodwill to every inhabitant, and it is robbed of its power to harm. [38] (Shinn 32-33)

How should the descendants of the enslaved Africans forgive and begin a healing process from the suffering as a result of the Trans-Atlantic Slave trade? As long as the effects and treatment of the descendants of the Africans forced into Slavery are detrimental, there will be a need to look into the past to correct the future. When you see a person of a different race or religion, do you form an immediate opinion of them before they utter one word? If it is negative, you may be fueling prejudice and stereotypes from learned behavior passed down by society. We are all guilty of it to some degree if we are honest with ourselves. The shackles of the Slave trade are ever present in society through racism, discrimination, segregation, and inequality especially towards people of African descent. Mental Slavery is just as toxic as physical Slavery. An awakening from God is the only way that prejudice, bigotry, and racism will finally come to an end. All believers in Christ possess the God given right through the authority of Jesus Christ to release them from the bondage of whatever has them bound.

Matt. 6:14-15 says, "For if you forgive others their trespasses, your heavenly Father will also forgive you; but if you do not forgive other, neither will your Father forgive your trespasses. [39] *(Matt. 6:14-15)*

There will always be individuals who through the passing of the torch of erroneous thinking accepted down through the centuries who will continue to think of themselves as superior and unfortunately feel they have the right to treat and judge people any way they please. It is too late for those who have passed on before us, God will judge them. But it is not too late for the living to change their minds and treatment of others. Exposure and the freedom to have dialogue will keep freedom and equality for all in view. The oppressed must walk upright with the power and the full armor of God, and the confidence of knowing that a person who seeks to control another human being in any form or fashion is an oppressor who does not have the right to do so.

Endnotes:

(7) Num. 1:18

(8) Holy Bible King James Version - Cain Hope Felder - James C. Winston Publishing - 1993 – (Page 334)

(9) Daniel Adjai-Ghanian tour guide

(10) *Isaiah 6:8*

(11) Special Issue, Fall/Winter - Tom Morganthau- Newsweek - 1991

(12) Ghana's slave castles causing controversy five centuries later - Beth Duff-Brown -   The Associated Press - 1997

(13) *Gen. 4:9-10*

(14) Special Issue, Fall/Winter - Tom Morganthau- Newsweek - 1991

(15) Magazine: History Today – August – 1999

(16) The History of The Trans Atlantic Slave Trade 1440-1870 - Hugh Thomas - Simon & Schuster Inc. – 1997 – (Page 1)

(17) New African - Patrick Adibe and Osei Boateng - March 2000 Issue (Page 24)

(18) Reversing Sail A History of the African Diaspora - Michael Gomez - Cambridge   University Press – 2005 (Page 122)

(19) Reversing Sail A History of the African Diaspora - Michael Gomez - Cambridge   University Press – 2005 (Page 127)

(20) *Holy Bible King James Version* - Cain Hope Felder - James C. Winston Publishing - 1993 – (Page 334)

(21) The abolition of the slave trade: Christian conscience and political action John Coffey – Vol. 15 No 2 June 2006

(22) The Atlantic Slave Trade - Herbert S. Klein - Cambridge University Press – (Page130)

(23) Islam's Black Slaves The other Black Diaspora - Ronald Segal - Farrar, Straus, and Giroux -1995 (Page 1)

(24) The abolition of the slave trade: Christian conscience and political action John Coffey – Vol. 15 No 2 June 2006

(25) Deut. 15:12-15

(26) Reversing Sail A History of the African Diaspora - Michael Gomez - Cambridge University Press – 2005 (Page 126)

(27) Answering Islam - Rev. Richard P. Bailey - 2004 – (Vol. 4)

(28) Beth Duff-Brown- The Associated Press - 1997

(29) Special Issue, Fall/Winter - Tom Morganthau- Newsweek - 1991

(30) *Matt. 22:34-40*

(31) African Chiefs Must Apologise For Slave Trade - Winston Tamakloe, Adaklu Kodzobi - Ghanaian Times News 2007 (Page 16)

(32) *Daniel 1: 6-7*

(33) *Holy Bible King James Version* - Cain Hope Felder - James C. Winston Publishing - 1993 – (Page 1254)

(34) YAA ASANTEWAA - Asirifi Danquah – Books Limited – 2002 (Page 2-3)

(35) Answering Islam - Rev. Richard P. Bailey - 2004 – (Vol. 4)

(36) Islam's Black Slaves The other Black Diaspora - Ronald Segal - Farrar, Straus, and Giroux -1995 (Page 9-10)

(37) Islam's Black Slaves The other Black Diaspora - Ronald Segal - Farrar, Straus, and Giroux -1995 (Page 8)

(38) Florence Scovel- Shinn - Simon & Schuster – 1925 – (Page 32-33)

(39) *Matt. 6:14-15*

CHAPTER III – RESEARCH

Connecting the Dots of Slavery

An endeavor to resolve the connection and responsibility of Christians and Christianity to the Trans-Atlantic Slave trade, and recount the unconscionable acts of the Slave trade was so important that additional journeys to Africa and Europe were essential to honor the history of the enslaved African Ancestors. Africans were sold for nothing that mattered, and were oppressed for no reasons that make any sense. Many enslaved African descendants mourn the loss of disconnect from their unknown families and heritage. In the end, God has the last word.

Who will break the chains of silence for the Christians' roles in the Trans-Atlantic Slave trade? Someone has to tell what happened to the African people taken against their will. Men, women, and children were forcibly taken from their villages and homes and forced to walk hundreds of miles to the Slave castles and forts. What happened behind the walls of the Slave castles and forts? There is a contentious responder to the call from Marlene, a descendant of two enslaved Africans named Charity from Sierra Leone or Liberia and Flora Slaver from an unknown African country.

What constitutes freedom? What truly sets men, women, and children free? What will set descendents of the enslaved Africans free? Whose version of the truth are we to believe? What portion of society do the African descendants fit into? Should the world simply forget what happened to the ancestors of the Slave trade? Where was the humanity instead of humiliation or compassion over cruelty? Discrimination, racism, and Slavery still exist, so the oppressed are not free. Humanity must be willing to move beyond stereotypical predisposed opinions of people they perceive to be different from themselves. If only people of the world could see beyond the color of one's skin and cultural differences. Then the energy of prejudice and hatred would transform into a peaceful world.

Isaiah 52:3-6 says, *"For thus says the LORD: You were sold for nothing, and you shall be redeemed without money. For thus says the LORD GOD: Long ago, my people went down into Egypt to reside there as aliens; the Assyrian, too, has oppressed them without cause. Now there what am I doing here, says the LORD, and continually, all day long, my name is despised. Therefore my people shall know my name; therefore in that day they shall know that it is I who speak; here am I."* [40] (Isaiah 52 3-6)

The woodcarving of the Volto Santo, "Holy Face" of Christ on the cross was discovered during my search for information on the Trans-Atlantic Slave trade in Italy. According to legend, the Volto Santo was carved by Nicodemus, a true eyewitness to the life and crucifixion of Christ. My breath was taken away, and I literally could not move at first glance. My husband and I had tears in our eyes and felt something in our hearts that could not be put into words. Jesus' face was one of compassion, even on the cross. I stared at the carving of our Lord and Savior Jesus the Christ hanging on the Cross for as long as possible, because I never wanted to forget what was being witnessed that day. There was a desire to capture every detail, especially the face and eyes. Nicodemus' work of love was the most important historical work of art that I might ever encounter. This revelation served as a confirmation for me from God that His will for this research project to be completed was in line with the teachings of Christ to set the oppressed free.

The Volto Santo" Holy Face" of Christ by Nicodemus is a precious historical religious masterpiece of Christian history as stated by our tour guide. Nicodemus finished all but the face of Christ, because he was not sure of the best way to capture it. While Nicodemus was asleep, the Holy face was divinely done. When Nicodemus awoke, the face of Christ was completed. The statue was discovered in the 8th century by pope Gualfredo. He decided to put it on a boat with no crew. Where ever the boat came to rest is where this precious gift was supposed to be. Pope Giovanni from Lucca was contacted by the person who

Lucca Italy Postcard of the Volto Santo "Holy Face"

found the woodcarving when the boat came to rest on the shore at Luni Italy. Pope Giovanni had the carving moved to Lucca and it was eventually placed at the San Martino Cathedral where it remains to date. The imprint of the Holy Face was put on the coins of Lucca. For centuries, pilgrimages from popes and others have been made to Lucca to pay respect and receive divine instructions and grace from contact with the Holy Face. The jewels that adorn the Prince of Peace are placed loving during the two yearly solemn festivals and are on display at San Martino. What was most disturbing is that one of the most significant pieces of Christian history has been for the most part hidden away!

The Cathedral of San Martino

Luke 4:18 says that Christ came to earth not only to encourage the poor, but He came to end slavery and set the oppressed free.

"The Spirit of the Lord is upon me, because he has anointed me to bring good news to the poor. He has sent me to proclaim

release to the captives and recovery of sight to the blind, to let the oppressed go free." [41] (Luke 4:18)

The following engraving on the grounds of the "Cradle of Civilization" historic site in South Africa ties all of humanity to African roots. So in essence, the Europeans and people of the Americas enslaved their own ancestors. What a thought!

Entrance to the Cradle of Civilization museum in South Africa

In the art and writings of European history, one might think that human civilization began in Europe. Dr. Louis Leakys' discoveries changed forever the erroneous teachings of whom and where mankind first began. Leaky proved that Africa was the Cradle of all Civilization. This truth makes Slavery even more appalling that people of African descent were and are treated so inhumanely.

"According to Dr. Leaky, the European paleontologist who discovered Lucy, the oldest set of human bones ever found on this planet, Africa is the birthplace of the human family. According to Mendel, the European scientist who proved that dark genes are dominant and light genes are recessive, Africans are the original people, and the parents of all human beings."[42] (Patriotic Vanguard)

The African American Heritage Hymnal contains an emotional humanitarian request to bring peace, harmony, and forgiveness to all man kind taught to us by God. God sent his Son Jesus Christ to reconcile us one to another. "Lord God, it was an African garden that you created the human family. Under watchful eye, Moses led your people out of Egypt while you guided your children through the wilderness. The Hebrew boys escaped the fiery furnace. Likewise, you guided African Americans through the perils of enslavement and brutality. Forgive those who accept ideas of racial inferiority and prejudice. Our leaders have taught us how to love in the face of hatred. We therefore seek reconciliation, and not revenge. We extend love and fellowship to all who, like us, are created in your image. God you sought to repair the damage done in the garden by sending your Son, Jesus Christ to reconcile us to you and to each other. Thank you for the ministry of reconciliation that lifts our spirits and changes our hearts. Help us to forgive those who need peace and healing, and grant us a clearer understanding of your truth. Give us courage to stand against those who would continue to sow evil and may our lives point others to respect, equality, and dignity."[43] (African American Heritage Hymnal 84)

Frequently asked questions for countless years regarding the Trans-Atlantic Slave Trade has been, why the Africans? What could possibly justify so many people being brutally enslaved mistreated and oppressed for so long? Deuteronomy 28:68 prophesied the African enslavement by way of ships. Millions of Africans were sold to their enemies as bondsmen and bondswomen and never returned home again.

"A Prophetic Return to Egypt" was prophesied in Deuteronomy 28:68. The prophetic statement made by God that the African Hebrews would be returned to Egypt again. But this time, "by way of ships… and there they would be sold unto their enemies for bondsmen and bondswomen…" It is certain that this prophecy fell upon only one people on the face of the earth, the people of Africa-the victims of the greatest, most cruel, vicious, and horrifying slave trade in the annals of history." [44] (Felder 334)

The Trans-Atlantic Slave trade began and continued for centuries with cruelty, greed, lies, and deceit. Who knew that the Slave trade would continue for almost four hundred years? It is no wonder that the Trans-Atlantic Slave trade crimes against humanity continues to remain controversial and unsettled. There are incessant efforts to defend the oppressed and reveal the suppressed history of the Slave trade.

"This is a moral universe, which means that despite all the evidence that seems to be to the contrary, there is no way that evil and injustice and oppression and lies can have the last word. ... that is what has upheld the orales of our people, to know that in the end good will prevail.

In a situation where human life seems dirt cheap, with people being killed as easily as one swats a fly, we must proclaim that people matter and matter enormously." [45] (Tutu 22)

The Europeans did not originally visit Africa for Slaves. They initially traded merchandise for gold, spices, rum, and molasses just to name a few. When the gold was depleted so the Europeans thought; the Slave trade was initiated. The first enslaved Africans from the Trans-Atlantic Slave trade were given as gifts to Prince Henry the Navigator of Portugal, as previously noted in Chapter I. How could human beings be given away as gifts? Some Africans were tricked into believing that they would return home after their work was completed at the Slave castles and forts. Decisions were made by Europeans regularly concerning the best ways to stack as many purchased Negroes as possible onto slaving ships.

"Year after year in quiet, calm office-rooms in a myriad of European seaports the thoughtful plans were laid. The aim of these plans was to make money; their result was the stacking of purchased Negroes in the holds of slaving ships, which transported them to a new county. There instead of the happy, limited life of the African villages they ground the slave barracks and the lash. There the sound of drums throbbing nightly in the vast African forest was exchanged for the pre-dawn summons to the can-fields at the squawk of the conch and for the melancholy tolling of the plantation bell." [46] (Hennessy 12)

The following description of white men arriving in ships with wings signaled danger and fear. The Europeans wasted no time in asserting authority over people that they never met before. Kidnappings and violence became their signature early on. Africans began running for their lives and have never stopped.

"One day the white men arrived in ships with wings, which shone in the sun like knives. They fought hard battles with the Ngola and spat fire at him. They conquered his saltpans and the Ngola fled inland to the Lukala River: -a Pende oral tradition (Congo) The Transatlantic Slave Trade was pioneered by the Portuguese in the 15th and 16th centuries. European exploration along the African coast began after Portugal captured Serta (or Ceuta, in Modern Morocco) from the Moors in 1415. To Europe, this "minor" victory at Ceuta was very significant indeed!"[47] (Tamakloe and Kodzobi)

Cunning Europeans encouraged wars among the people of Africa to get them to turn against one another, thereby considering each others as enemies. The divide and conquering methods assisted with Africans selling their own people, because they did not consider them as their own. Unfortunately the divide and conquer brain washing passed down through the centuries continues to exist among many people of Africa and throughout the Diaspora today.

"Slave traders actively encouraged wars in Africa, resulting in the death or enslavement of millions more Africans on that continent than ended up in the Americas. Scholars of African history believe the total number of Africans killed or abducted in Africa and the Americas could be between 50 and 100 million. Whatever the figure, the slave trade brought death and dislocation on an unimaginable scale. Its full impact will never be fully known." [48] (Mariners' Museum)

There are different explanations for why Slavery began on the continent of Africa. Some are provided in this chapter. The reasons were significant and worth every life in the Slavers opinions, but the motives for Slavery taking so long to end came down to control, revenge, greed, and lust of money.

"It is extraordinary that, considering that less than 5% of all the Trans Atlantic slaves ended up in North America, the vast majority of films, books and articles concerning the slave trade concentrate only on the American involvement in the slave trade, as though slavery was a uniquely American aberration. However, the vastly greater involvement of Portugal, Spain and France seem to be largely ignored. Even more so the far greater and longer running Islamic slave trade into the Middle East has been so ignored as to make it one of history's best-kept secrets." [49] (Christian Action Magazine)

The Slave trade was blamed for permanently weakening the African continent. This theory is believed by many, as stated by Elikia M'bokolo

"Of all these slave routes, the "slave trade" in its purest form, i.e. the European Atlantic trade, attracts most attention and gives rise to most debate. The Atlantic trade is the least poorly documented to date, but this is not the only reason. More significantly, it was directed at Africans only, whereas the Muslim countries enslaved both Blacks and Whites. And it was the form of slavery that indisputably contributed most to the present situation of Africa. It permanently weakened the continent, led to its colonization by the Europeans in the nineteenth century, and engendered the racism and contempt from which Africans still suffer." [50] (M'bokolo)

Who was Involved in the Slave Trade?

There has been more controversy and conversation surrounding when the Slave trade actually began, and by whom as opposed to the deaths, devastation, and permanent destruction forced on the Africans and the ravaging of Africa's natural resources. The year 1444 seems to be the one most mentioned to signify the official start of the Trans-Atlantic Slave trade. Just as the history of the United States of America acquaints its discovery with Christopher Columbus, the start of Slavery mentions Christopher Columbus as well.

"But, while the year 1441, or even 1444, may be taken as making the beginning of the slave trade the most significant year in its history in the year 1493, when Christopher Columbus discovered the New World. For the next three and a half centuries and at ever-increasing momentum, the development of the new territories across the Atlantic demanded millions upon millions of African slaves. The Americas, and the sugar island of the Caribbean, became as insatiable as the great god Baal himself." [51] (Hennessy 12)

This statue of Christopher Columbus in Barcelona Spain was commissioned by Queen Isabella and King Ferdinand honoring Columbus for his discoveries of new lands, and dedicated service

Christopher Columbus was involved in the Slave trade starting with his first voyage in 1492. It is believed that he served as a deck hand on one of the Slave ships that docked at Elmina Slave Castle on the Cape Coast of Ghana. His voyage carried sugar cane which was one of the main reasons for so many enslaved Africans arrival in the Caribbean. The Spaniards prospered from the Slave trade, and it stands to reason that Columbus did also.

"The location of these islands made them a principal supply base for ships heading across the Atlantic, starting with Columbus's first voyage in 1492. Sugar cane was first carried to the Caribbean and Americas from the Canaries on a return voyage in 1493 to Santo Domingo, and the first shipment cultivated by enslaved Africans was returned to Spain in 1516. Although never a rival to Seville, the merchants and sailors of the Canaries prospered greatly by investing in slavery in the Americas." [52] (Anti Slavery)

A Spanish priest was responsible for Africans being shipped to Hispaniola as Slaves. He wanted injustice and killings to stop for one class of people at the expense and enslavement of the African people.

"In later years, Spanish priest Bartolomew de Las Casas, fought against the massacre of the Indians and demanded that the injustices committed every day against the indigenous people in Hispaniola was stopped. And as a way of ending this form of indigenous slavery, he strongly encouraged the importation of Blacks from Africa to work on the mines. So, it was partly due to him, that in 1503, the first Africans were brought to Hispaniola as slaves."

"The Casa de Contratación (House of Trade) was set up in Seville in 1503, granting the city the exclusive right to trade with American colonies. These lands were considered the personal property of the Spanish monarchy, and the authorities in Seville were given the job of maximising profits for the royal treasury. All ships bound for the Americas had to leave and return to its docks, and as the undisputed centre of commerce in Spain it became one of Europe's biggest slave ports. The Tobacco Factory, built between 1728 and 1771 was designed to process the crop grown by enslaved Africans in the Spanish Caribbean. The largest industrial complex ever built in Spain by that time, it reflects the huge profits made from the enslavement of African peoples." [53] (Anti Slavery)

Spain Tobacco Factory "www.antislavery.org"

Enslaved Africans were referred to as a bumper harvest, not human beings by the Portuguese. The regents split the Africans into fifths. What did they do if the numbers were not equal? The Regents tried to present themselves as savers of the Africans' souls.

"By 1444 one of several subsequent expeditions brought back a bumper harvest of two hundred and thirty-five African men, women and children who, landed at the Portuguese port of Lagos, were then disembarked and herded together in a meadow outside the city walls. Here they were parceled out into lots under the benign eye of the Regent of Portugal who rode out to watch the proceedings mounted on a thoroughbred horse. The Regent's share of the captives was one fifth of the whole, and these he redistributed amongst his retinue. The contemporary chronicler of the scene records the 'great pleasure' with which the pious Regent 'reflected ...upon the salvation of those souls that before were lost'. The choicest of the Africans were presented as an offering to the chief church of Lagos, and one little boy was sent to St Vincent do Cabo to be educated. He grew up a Franciscan friar." [54] (Hennessy 8-9)

Even worse was the capture of Africans with fish hooks and treating them worse than fish to keep them from swimming away and escaping the horrors and torment that awaited them.

"But it was not all easy for the Portuguese kidnappers. Gomes Eannes Zurara recorded that: "Our men had great toil in the capture of those who where swimming, for they dived like cormorants, so that they could not get hold of them; and the capture of the second man caused them to lose all the others. For he was so valiant that two [Portuguese] men, strong as they were, could not drag him into the boat until they took a boat-hook and caught him above one eye, and the pain of this made him abate his courage, and allow himself to be put inside the boat." [55] (Thomas 24)

The Portuguese used trading merchandise and religion as reasons for their involvement with certain tribes in the Kongo. The following letter was a desperate plea for the King of Portugal to send missionaries and other religious items and no goods for trade as further enticements for the tribesmen. Prayerfully this request would stop the brutal kidnappings.

"Each day the traders are kidnapping our people-children of this country, sons of our nobles and vassals, even people of our own family. This corruption and depravity are so widespread that our land is entirely depopulated. We need in this kingdom only priest and schoolteachers, and no merchandise, unless it is wine and flour for Mass. It is our wish that this Kingdom not be a place for the trade or transport of slaves.

Many of our subjects early lust after Portuguese merchandise that your subjects have brought into our domains. To satisfy this inordinate appetite, they seize many of our black free subjects.... They sell them. After having taken these prisoners to the coast secretly or at night.... As soon as the captives are in the hands of white men they are branded with a red-hot iron." [56] (Hochschild)

Sierra Leone is significant to the history of enslaved African descendants in America, and Britain. Many of the enslaved Africans shipped from the west coast of Africa to America and Liverpool England were from Sierra Leone and Liberia.

The kidnappings of Africans from that region and trading of the people for goods such as rum and molasses took place early on during the Slave trade.

"This unusual scheme," says Hugh Thomas, "was remarkably successful. Starting form Sierra Leone, captains sailing under Gomes' directions swiftly found what became known as the Grain Coast (southern Sierra Leone and what is now Liberia), and then, sailing directly east, the Cote d'Ivoire (Cape Palmas to Cape Three Points); and the coast that the Portuguese at first called El Mina (which may be a corruption of "A Mina" the mine in Portuguese, but more likely to come from "El Minnah", Arabic for "the port", because here they were at last close to gold mines, those of the Akan forest [of Ghana]..." [57] (Adibe and Boateng 24)

"The British traders based at Bunce island shipped thousands of Africans captives to South Carolina, Georgia, Florida, and other Southern Colonies during the mid-and late 1700s. Rice planters in South Carolina and Georgia were particularly anxious to buy captives from Sierra Leone and other parts of the "Rice Coast" where Africans have grown rice for thousands of years. Slave auction advertisements in 18th century Charles Town (South Carolina) and Savannah (Georgia) often mentioned ships arriving with slaves brought from the "Rice Coast, "Sierra-Leon,: and "Bance Island." African farmers taken from the Rice Coast region made rice one of the most profitable industries in early America." [58] (BBC)

More than one date has been suggested to signify the Dutch involvement in the Slave trade. The government officials haggled over allowing Slave markets to exist. Over the years, the Dutch became some of the biggest offenders of the Slave trade and profited greatly from it.

"One of the earliest direct Dutch connections with the African slave trade occurred in 1596, when a Rotterdam skiper, Pieter van der Haagen, brought 130 African slaves into the harbor of Middelburg, capital of the province of Zeeland. After lengthy debates, the city council decided that no slave market would be allowed there and that the slaves should be released and allowed to find jobs as free laborers. Similar incidents had taken place in Amsterdam in connection with the Portuguese Jews residing in that city, which suggest that the Dutch themselves were not favorably disposed to enter the trade in humans beings, which was widely practiced in southern European cities at the time.

This attitude prevailed until 1621, when the Dutch West India Company (West-Indisch Compagnie, hereafter referred to as WIC), came into being. Some of the shareholders suggested participation in the slave trade; however, after consultation with theologians the directors agreed that the trade in human beings was moraly not justified and should therefore not be practiced by the company."[59] (Thomas 10-11)

The Dutch West India Company, (WIC) was the largest single Slave trader in Europe. The greed of their shareholders won the arguments in favor of the Slave trade. Amsterdam was the

Dutch capital of the Slave trade. The change of heart of the shareholders did not come prior to the Dutch accumulating massive wealth that their ancestors are still benefiting from centuries later. Amsterdam was also the capital of Slavery in Europe. The Banking systems in Europe profited tremendously from the Slave trade.

"West-Indisch Huis (West Indies House, see photo below) in the centre of Amsterdam was the former headquarters of the Dutch West-Indische Compagnie (West India Company or WIC), which was probably the largest single slave trader in history. The company was chartered in 1621, and provided with a monopoly on the African slave trade that lasted until 1730. This building was occupied from 1621-1647, a period which saw the first of 30,000 slaves arriving in Dutch Brazil, arranged through the WIC.

Amsterdam ranks as a European capital of slavery. While its mills processed almost all the sugar from the Portuguese colonies, its financiers bankrolled the Danish, Swedish and Brandenburg slave trade, and in turn Scandinavian and German sailors made up half its slaving crews. As home to the world's most sophisticated banking and insurance system, it was the natural home for the expensive and potentially risky business of slaving, and for this reason alone as many as 10,000 vessels were associated with the port." [60] (Anti Slavery)

The French participation in the Slave trade was horrendous. Louis XIV signed for the horrible treatment of Africans with "The Code Noir". The provision for the mutilation of Africans was considered the humanitarian portion of the regulations. Yet the branding, or beating, or flogging was considered humane, because these methods of violence were allowed. Even though slavery was abolished during the French revolution, Napoleon reestablished its legitimacy. The following information revealing the monetary gains of the French from the Slave trade encouraged their greed.

"The Code Noir was signed by Louis XIV in 1685 to provide formal regulations for slavery, and became the template for ruling slavery in other French colonies like Louisiana (in the US). It defined slaves as 'portable property', and laid out an extremely harsh and rigid system of discipline and restrictions. It did however include certain humanitarian provisions, in part to control the slave mutilation that was so widespread in the French Caribbean. It enforced Catholic worship, provided religious holidays and instruction, tolerated intermarriage, attempted to preserve families and offered a modicum of protection for slaves. It was a brutal system, punishing even minor crimes with branding and flogging, and importantly gave the human trade a legitimate legal status. It was briefly abolished during the revolution, but restored by Napoleon. King Louis Phillipe gradually dismantled the system over the 1830s.

Although most French slaves were taken from West Africa for the Transatlantic Slave Trade, a limited trade existed in the Indian Ocean. 50,000 people were abducted from Madagascar and Mozambique to work the sugar plantations of Bourbon (now Réunion) and Ile de France (Mauritius). The trade reached a peak in the islands under Napoleonic rule (1803-1815), due to reforms of commerce and the profits drawn from captured English ships." [61] (The National library of France, Paris)

Scathing Accusations

A legal basis in favor of Slavery was argued by Sir Edward Coke of England. Coke was credited with giving Slavery legitimacy in English colonies in England and America. Coke helped write the charter of the Virginia Company. His arguments were used as an excuse by Queen Elizabeth for not apologizing for England's participation in the Trans-Atlantic Slave trade.

"Sir Edward Coke (pronounced "cook") "(1 February 1552 - 3 September 1634) was an early English colonial entrepreneur and jurist whose writings on the English common law were the definitive legal texts for some 300 years. He is credited with having established the legal basis for Slavery in the English colonies.

In 1606, Coke helped write the charter of the Virginia Company, a private venture granted a royal charter to found settlements in North America. He became directory of the London Company, one of the two branches of the Virginia Company. As director, he proposed a means by which Slavery could be legalised in the new Virginia Colony. Fearing opposition if the issue was publicly debated, Coke was responsible for Calvin's Case in 1608, which ruled that "all infidels are in law perpetual enemies". Here he was borrowing from a legal tradition rooted in canonical law and apologetics for the crusades. In this way Coke played a significant part in the development of New World Slavery."
[62] (Bowan)

Not only was the Royal family of Britain directly involved in the Trans-Atlantic Slave trade, King Charles II was a supporter of it. Power over the Slave trade was supported and directed by Lord Mayors, and sheriffs that were also involved. So if there was involvement from the throne to the law, the Africans and the minority few who believed Slavery was wrong had to fight hundreds of years to end it. The problem is, by that time the Britain coiffures and the infrastructure including major banking systems were tainted with the blood of innocent human beings that cannot be erased.

"The financial involvement of the Royal family and the country's aristocracy were central to the growth of Britain's slave trade and the slaving company known as the Royal Adventurers into Africa (1660) counted King Charles II as a backer. A later corporation - the Royal African Company - founded in 1672, made London the only English city that would benefit from the slave trade until 1698. The Royal African Company set up and administered trading posts on the west African coast, and was responsible for seizing any English ships - other than its own - which were involved in slaving ventures. This stranglehold of the slave traders and plantation owners over the City of London was very powerful. 15 Lord Mayors of London, 25 sheriffs and 38 aldermen of the City of London were shareholders in the Royal African Company between 1660-1690." [63] (Anti Slavery)

One of Britain's major cities Liverpool was the place where the majority of the enslaved Africans arrived from Sierra Leone and other West African coastal countries. The major banks owners and council members were very much involved in the Trans-Atlantic Slave Trade.

'Liverpool is arguably the city in Britain that was most complicit in the slave trade. By 1750, 10 of Liverpool's 14 most prominent banks were owned by slave traders. By 1787, 37 of the 41 members of the Liverpool council were involved in some way in slavery. Further, all of Liverpool's 20 Lord Mayors who held office between 1787 and 1807 were involved. Today their names are engraved in one of the huge bronze plaques, which dominates the Liverpool Town Hall's main committee room. This 18th century building speaks volumes about the city's trade links, a close inspection of its carvings revealing elephants, lions, crocodiles and African faces." [64] (Anti Slavery)

The American Revolutionary War is most often associated with Americas' independence, but it was also about the Slave trade being tied into America's independence from Britain. The Slave Castle Bunce Island was British owned. Laurens, the man who became the President of the Continental Congress and negotiated in part the U.S. Independence was heavily involved in the Trans-Atlantic Slave trade. Take a look at the deal that was cut between America and Britain, and how the Slave trade played a significant role in the following paragraph. Let's face it; America supposedly the land of the free was tainted with enslaved African Blood from the beginning.

"Henry Laurens, a wealthy South Carolina slave dealer and rice planter, was Bunce Island's business agent in Charles Town before the American Revolutionary War. After the war began, Laurens became the President of the Continental Congress, and when the fighting finally ended, he was named one of the American Peace Commissioners who negotiated U.S. Independence under the Treaty of Paris. In other words, United States Independence as negotiated, in part, between Bunce Island's British owner and his American business agent in South Carolina. The relationship between these two men reflects the importance in the commerce that linked Britain, North American, and West Africa during the Colonial Period" [65] (BBC)

M'bokolo provides a good synopsis of what happened as a result of the Europeans and others tricking Africans with using Christianity as a sag way into getting tribal Chiefs and Kings in Africa to participate in the Slave trade and the European colonization of African countries.

"Why the Africans rather than other peoples? Who exactly should be held responsible for the slave trade? The Europeans alone, or the Africans themselves? Did the slave trade do real damage to Africa, or was it a marginal phenomenon affecting only a few coastal societies?

The great slaving companies were formed in the second half of the seventeenth century, when the Americas, and other parts of the world which the Treaty of Tordesillas (1494) and various papal edicts had reserved to the Spaniards and Portuguese, were redistributed among the nations of Europe. The whole of Europe - France, England, Holland, Portugal and Spain, and even Denmark, Sweden and Brandenburg shared in the spoils, establishing a chain of monopoly companies, forts, trading posts and colonies that stretched from Senegal to Mozambique. Only distant Russia and the Balkan countries were missing from the pack - and they received their own small contingents of slaves via the Ottoman Empire.

In Africa itself, sporadic raids by Europeans soon gave way to regular commerce. African societies were drawn into the slavery system under duress, hoping that, once inside it, they would be able to derive maximum benefit for themselves. Nzinga Mbemba, ruler of the Kongo Kingdom, is a good example. He had converted to Christianity in 1491 and referred to the king of Portugal as his brother. When he came to power in 1506, he protested strongly at the fact that the Portuguese, his brother's subjects, felt entitled to rob his possessions and carry off his people into slavery. It was to no avail." [66] (M'bokolo)

The renowned European Calvinist theologians who spoke out against Slavery were in the minority. The majority of them accepted or found ways to legitimize Slavery for money, using scripture to justify their thinking.

"In general, Calvinist theologians accepted slavery as a ligitimate human institution, justifying it on the so-called curse of Ham theory, which held that blacks were the offspring of Ham (and his son Canaan), the son of the biblical Noah, who had dishonored his father and thereby drew a curse of God that condemned his offspring to perpetual servitude. Calvinist who spoke out against slavery in the pre-eighteenth-century Enlightenment days were the exception to the rule. It is therefore quite likely that the majority of the WIC directors were economically motivated in selecting particular Calvinist advisers who would give them the advice they wished to hear." [67] (Thomas 11)

It really doesn't matter if they were new Christians or old

Christians, the problem is that a great number of Christians were involved in the Trans-Atlantic Slave trade. It seemed as if Christians believed in Christ, but not His teachings. Christians allowed greed and arrogance to blind their obligation to protect and not use and abuse their fellowmen.

"Old Christians were also engaged in the slave traffic in Seville: there was, for example, not only Juan de la Barrera, mentioned in the last chapter, but Rodrigo de Gabraleon' of Seville, who was concerned with pearls as well as slaves. His son Antonio acted as his agent in Nombre de Dios, where he stayed till 1550, when his father died." [68] (Thomas 128)

The Slave trade was opposed by some Christians because of the cruelty by many Slave traders and owners. Shamefully more Christians accepted Slavery because they traded and or owned Slaves themselves.

"British slave trading had begun in the late sixteenth century, and grew apace during the seventeenth and eighteenth centuries. By 1807, around three million slaves had been transported to the Americas on British ships. The trade was occasionally denounced by Christians. Richard Baxter declared that slave-traders were 'fitter to be called devils than Christians', and the Puritan Samuel Sewall published America's first antislavery tract, *The Selling of Joseph* (1700). But most Christians in the early eighteenth century accepted slavery as a fact of life. The evangelist George Whitefield deplored the cruelty of slave-owners in the American South, but did not condemn slavery itself – indeed, he owned over fifty slaves in Georgia." [69] (Coffey 2006)

The universal opinion of clergy and Christians' belief that God ordained Slavery was a way for them to justify owning them. This included Sir John Hawkins who named one of his Slave ships Angel. They went as far as amputating the captive's legs to prevent them from escaping. What messages were they delivering to parishioners on Sundays regarding the treatment of one's fellow man? They were supposedly devout men of great respect.

"The record of the Anglican Church was no better than that of the Roman Church. It was the universal opinion of churchmen that God had ordained slavery, and clergymen had no qualms about owning slaves themselves. Anglican slave traders were often extremely devout, and widely respected by their fellow Christians. It never occurred to them, or to their priests or ministers that slave trading might be immoral. The most famous English slave trader, Sir John Hawkins, piously named his slave ships Angel, Jesus, and Grace of God.

Since they were merely property, there could be no objection to branding slaves just like any other animal. Neither was there any obligation to treat them more humanely than animals in other ways. Their prices depended on supply and demand like any other commodity. Female breeders would be sold at a premium prices after the importation of African slaves to North America and the Caribbean ceased. Sometimes slaves were hamstrung to stop them escaping. If they had escaped before, they could have a leg amputated to stop them doing so again. Once their working lives were over, they were put-down." [70] (Awake)

1Timothy 1:8-10 states what will happen to those who disobey the word of God, including slave traders. It proves that God was against the Slave traders and therefore against Slavery.

"Now we know that the law is good. If one uses it legitimately. This means understanding that the law is laid down not for the innocent but for the lawless and disobedient, for the godless and sinful, for the unholy and profane. For those who kill their father or mother, for murderers, fornicators, sodomites, slave traders, liars, perjurers, and whatever else is contrary to the sound teaching that is contrary to the sound teaching." [71] *(1Timothy 1:8-10)*

Europeans usually made disparaging remarks about Africans as stated by Adibe and Boateng. Even when they found ways to place the blame on the Africans themselves, it did not erase Europeans assigning horrible stereotypes to the people they took advantage of. Professor Clarke provides information pertaining to the beginning of the Slave trade that is not in the history books, and why Africans sold their own people into Slavery.

"Contrary to the many traveler's takes told by Europeans about African being "no better than beast", and who "lived in trees" in those days, the Europeans in fact came to meet civilised, structured societies in Africa.

So why did the African who' lived in civilised, structured societies," agree to sell their own people to the Europeans? The African American historian, Prof Clarke, appears to have the best answer. In his lecture in London in 1988, he said:

"Your history books tell you that a major event happened in 1492, but something else happened within Africa in that year that Africans need to pay some attention to also.

"In 1492, Sonni Ali, emperor of one of the last great African nations in West Africa, Songhay, was drowned on his way home from a battle in the south. He had been an able ruler and his conflict with the priest was over religion."

After Sonni Ali's death, a scramble for power ensued for a whole year in Songhay. A commoner, Mohammed Abu Biki Ituri, came to power as a result of the Scramble. "He created the last of the great dynasties of the independent African nation-states before the encroachment of the slave trade that spread inland into Africa," said Prof Clark. "This is the last of the great African nation-states, covered a massive area larger than the continental limits of the United States...

Said Prof Clarke: "There is something a scholar of this period must understand, because it is true: Except for the drain of Africa's time and resources brought home by the Arab slave trade and the Arabs in general, Africa could have had enough strength and organisation to resist the European slave trade." [72] (Adibe and Boateng 26)

The disenfranchisement of great kingdoms like Dahomey brought to an end the great histories of many African dynasties. Europeans stole the land and the people, and kidnapped Kings and Queens. Many of the great leaders were forced into Slavery and or had their titles reduced to Chief to keep their titles from being on the same levels as European royalty.

"Dahomey (its capital is Abomey) was an important

kingdom in Benin's history. Many enslaved Africans left from here during the 16-18th centuries. It was a strong military empire, and feared by its neighbours. Legend says that the 'founder' of the three main kingdoms in southern Benin (Allada, Dahomey, and Porto-Novo) were from the same family, sometime in the 1500s, from a village near the Mono River, in what is now Togo. This is a photo of King Agoli-Agbo, the last King of Dahomey from 1894-1901. He eventually signed a protectorate treaty, which considerably limited his powers and reduced him to a traditional Chief. He was soon deported and Danhomé was integrated into the colony of Dahomey. " [73] (Abomey Historical Museum)

King Agoli-Agbo www.antislavery.org

Because of the Color of Their Skin

The horrible and insensitive descriptions of Africans by Zurara is an example of just a few depictions of African features and physiques by Europeans and others that unfortunately continues to fuel racism towards Africans and enslaved African descendants presently. There was no humanity, dignity, or decency at anytime during the Slave trade in most situations.

"VERY EARLY in the morning, because of the heat', a few Portuguese seamen on the decks of half a dozen hundred-ton caravels, the new sailing ships, were preparing, on 8 August 1444, to land their African cargo near Lagos, on the south-west point of the Algarve, in Portugal.

The cargo consisted of 235 slaves. On arriving on the mainland, these people were placed in a field. They seemed, as a contemporary put it, 'a marvelous sight, for, amongst them, were some white enough, fair enough, and well-proportioned; others were less white, like mulattos; others again were as black Ethops, and so ugly, both in features and in body, as almost to appear... the images of a lower hemisphere.

'What heart could be so hard', this contemporary chronicler, Gomes Eannes de Zurara, a courtier attached to the brother of the King of Portugal, the inventive Prince Henry, asked himself,' as not to be pierced with piteous feeling to see that company? For some kept their heads low, and their faces bathed in tears, looking one upon another. Others stood groaning very dolorously, looking up to the height of heaven, fixing their eyes upon it, crying out loudly, as if asking help from the Father of nature; others struck their faces with the palms of their hands, throwing themselves at full length upon the ground; while others made lamentations in the manner of a dirge, after the custom of their country...'" [74] (Thomas 21-22)

Brutally Beaten and Tortured Enslaved African

An enslaved African sick child was compared to a calf slaughtered by a butcher in an excerpt from Fanny Trollope's writings about the manners of Americans.

"The author is nursing a slave girl who has accidentally taken poison. "I...took the little sufferer in my lap. I observed a general titter among the white members of the family...The youngest of the family, a little girl about the age of the young slave, after gazing at me for a few moments in utter astonishment, exclaimed: 'My! If Mrs. Trollope has not taken her in her lap, and wiped her nasty mouth! Why I would not have touched her mouth for two hundred dollars'...The idea of really sympathising in the sufferings of a slave appeared to them as absurd as weeping over a calf that had been slaughtered by the butcher." Excerpt from Fanny Trollope's Domestic Manners of the Americans."[75] (Trollope)

What impudence of the Portuguese for assuming that it was a minor inconvenience to the African families separated not by their own choosing and without thought, or conscious, or consideration. The Portuguese forever changed the face and future of the Africans that they kidnapped. To suggest that Africans should have been grateful for being well treated according to categorizations by the Portuguese. The Africans were taken in by Portuguese families and petted like dogs. The Portuguese really did not have a clue as to the havoc they placed upon the lives of enslaved Africans or their descendants, nor did they care.

"Except for the fact that families were torn apart, and the state of terror in which the enslaved Negroes at first gazed upon this strange white man's country, these early captives were well-treated, baptized, and absorbed into Portuguese households where they were petted and educated. Soon as it was realized that they were a musical people, it became fashionable for some of the great families of Lisbon to entertain their guest with African bands." [76] (Hennessy 9)

The reference referring to Africans as "these people" is a negative connotation that is very offensive and implies that Africans were not human.

"These people are in no way inferior to the Dutch as regards cleanliness; they wash and scrub their houses so well that they are polished and shinning like a looking-glass." [77] (Adibe and Boateng)

Unmitigated Profits

Most of the financing of historic buildings, bridges, and other commercial ventures was possible because of the free labor of the enslaved Africans forced to build them and the profits gained from the sale of Africans in France and other places throughout Europe and America.

"The slave trade greatly contributed to the town's immense commercial power, and prompted lavish projects to expand and luxuriously develop the town. Modern tourist sites like l'hotel de la Bourse and La Grosse Horloge (shown below), still dominate the port's skyline, and owe much of their splendour to the huge profits drawn from enslaving Africans. From the 16th Century La Rochelle expanded rapidly due to its trade with the colonies. In 1594 the ship L'Espérance (meaning 'hope') which was registered at this port, became the first French ship to be identified as participating in the slave trade. By the late 18th Century slavers made up a full third of the traffic which passed between the medieval towers of the Old Port." [78] (Anti Slavery)

France – LaRochelle (www.anti slavery.com)

As the Portuguese death toll mounted, King Henry decided to change tactics. He instructed one of his slave captains, Joao Fernandes, to change the superstructure of the Portuguese slavery. Instead of kidnapping the Africans, Fernandes should buy them, King Henry ordered. That changed the face of the Transatlantic Slave Trade forever." [79] (Adibe and Boateng 24-25)

The lives of Africans were exchanged for as little as salt, mangos, and cola nuts. In Sierra Leone, a mother and son were purchased for a basin and bracelets. The only reason King Henry of Portugal decided to purchase Africans toward the end of their control of the Slave trade was because of the number of Portuguese that died or were murdered in the process of kidnapping Africans.

"Slave buying was lucrative simply because the slavers got the slaves for next to nothing. For example, a mother and her son were brought in Sierra Leone in 1475, "for a barber's basin and three large bronze bracelits". (Adibe and Osei Boateng 26)[80]

Endnotes:

(40) Isaiah 52 3-6

(41) Luke 4:18

(42) The Patriotic Vanguard - Sierra Leone Portal - Monday December 4 2006

(43) African American Heritage Hymnal – GIA Publications, Inc. 2001 (Page 84)

(44) Holy Bible King James Version - Cain Hope Felder - James C. Winston Publishing - 1993 (Page 334)

(45) Believe the Words and Inspirations of Desmond Tutu- Blue Mountain Press - 2007 (page 22)

(46) The Atlantic Slave Traders 1441-1807 James Pope-Hennessy - Castle Books - 1967 – (Page 12)

(47) African Chiefs Must Apologise For Slave Trade – Winston Tamakloe, Adaklu   Kodzobi - Ghanaian Times News 2007 (Page 16)

(48) The Mariners' Museum – 2002

(49) Christian Action Magazine - South Africa - 2004

(50) The Impact of the Slave Trade on Africa Elikia M'bokolo – Le Monde Diplomatique - April 2, 1998

(51) The Atlantic Slave Traders 1441-1807 James Pope-Hennessy – Castle Books - 1967 – (Page 12)

(52) Breaking the Silence www.antislavery.org All Rights

Reserved - Ghana.co.uk - 1999-2001

(53) Breaking the Silence www.antislavery.org All Rights
Reserved. - Ghana.co.uk - 1999-2001

(54) The Atlantic Slave Traders 1441-1807 James Pope-Hennessy
- Castle Books - 1967 – (Page 8-9)

(55) The History of the Trans Atlantic Slave Trade 1440-1870 -
Hugh Thomas - Simon & Schuster Inc. – 1997 – (Page 24)

(56) King Leopold's Ghost: A Story of Greed, Terror, and Heroism
in Colonial Africa –   Adam Hochschild – Houghton Mifflin
Books - 1999

(57) Portugal, the mother of all slavers Part 1 New African –
Patrick Adibe and Osei Boateng - March 2000 Issue - (Page 24)

(58) www.antislavery.com-BBC.co.uk- last updated - January 22,
2007

(59) The History of the Trans Atlantic Slave Trade 1440-1870 -
Hugh Thomas - Simon & Schuster Inc. – 1997 – (Page 10-11)

(60) www.antislavery.com-BBC.co.uk- last updated - January 22,
2007

(61) The National Library of France, Paris

(62) The Lion and the Throne, a biography of Coke February 1552
3 September - 1634- Catherine Drinker Bowen - April 1990

(63) Breaking the Silence www.antislavery.org All Rights
Reserved. (Ghana.co.) - 1999-2001

(64) Breaking the Silence www.antislavery.org All Rights

Reserved. (Ghana.co.) - 1999-2001

(65) www.antislavery.com-BBC.co.uk - last updated - January 22, 2007

(66) The impact of the slave trade on Africa Elikia M'bokolo – Le Monde *diplomatique* - April 2, 1998

(67) The History of The Trans Atlantic Slave Trade 1440-1870 - Hugh Thomas - Simon & Schuster Inc. – 1997 – (Page 11)

(68) The History of The Trans Atlantic Slave Trade 1440-1870 - Hugh Thomas - Simon & Schuster Inc. – 1997 – (Page 128)

(69) The Abolition of The Slave Trade: Christian conscience and political action John Coffey – Vol. 15 No 2 - June 2006

(70) Awake Watch Tower Bible and Tract Society - September 8, 2001

(71) *1Timothy 1:8-10*

(72) New African - Patrick Adibe and Osei Boateng - March 2000 Issue - (Page 26)

(73) Abomey Historical Museum, Benin. www.epa-prema.net

(74) The History of The Trans Atlantic Slave Trade 1440-1870 - Hugh Thomas - Simon & Schuster Inc. – 1997 – (Page 21-22)

(75) Domestic Manners of the Americans Dramatization – Fannie Trollope BBC - February 1997

(76) The Atlantic Slave Traders 1441-1807 James Pope-Hennessy - Castle Books - 1967 – (Page 9)

(77) Portugal, the mother of all slavers Part 1 New African - Patrick Adibe and Osei Boateng - March 2000 Issue - (Page 24)

(78) Breaking the Silence www.antislavery.org All Rights Reserved. (Ghana.co) - 1999-2001

(79) Portugal, the mother of all slavers Part 1 New African - Patrick Adibe and Osei Boateng - March 2000 Issue - (Page 24)

(80) Portugal, the mother of all slavers Part 1 New African - Patrick Adibe and Osei Boateng - March 2000 Issue - (Page 26)

Chapter IV Research

Historic Slave Sites in Africa

Although there were more Slave castles, forts, and other human warehouses than should ever have existed, the sites visited will be the main focus of this chapter. The human warehouses hold the keys to the ancestral history of millions of enslaved Africans that never made it out of Africa or who were shipped during the middle passage of the Trans-Atlantic Slave trade. The sites that were visited are prefaced with an asterisk (*), detailed descriptions, and pictures. What John 8:32 says is one of the main reasons for completing this dissertation.

"Then you will know the truth and the truth will set you free." [81] (John 8:32)

*Goree Island - Maison des Esclaves or The Slave House

Goree Island - Maison des Esclaves, was mentioned in chapter one. It was the first Slave Castle my husband and I visited in Africa. The door of no return is most significant, because many of the enslaved Africans were shipped to America. Untold numbers of them choose to jump to their death rather than becoming a Slave. It is also one of the most frequently visited Slave sites outside of Ghana.

"This is the Maison des Esclaves or The Slave House. It was built in 1776 by the Dutch, and is one of several sites on the island where Africans were brought to be loaded onto ships bound for the New World. The owner's residential quarters were on the upper floor. The lower floor was reserved for the enslaved Africans who were weighed, fed and held before they were taken on the Middle Passage across the Atlantic. The Maison des Esclaves, with its famous "Door of No Return" has been preserved in its original state." [82] (Anti Slavery)

Courtyard of Goree Island Castle

Marlene stands in the Door of No Return, with the ocean below
as Evelyn and guide Abduli await their turn

Bill and Marlene on a balcony at the Goree' Island Slave Castle
after standing in the Door of No Return

Shekels and Weapons from the Slave trade, Plaque dedicated to
enslaved African Ancestors connected to Goree" Island

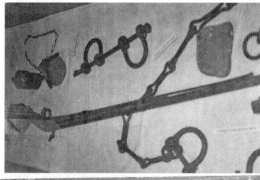

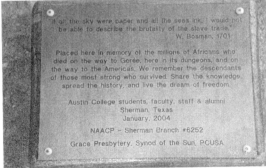

*The Slave Lodge in Cape Town South Africa

Unfortunately while visiting Cape Town South Africa, the Slave Lodge was not open. I was lead to believe by my tour guide that the museum did not contain enough information on the Slave trade for me to spend any time there. I later discovered that there was a great deal of Slave trade history connected to the Slave Lodge.

"The Slave Lodge is one of the oldest buildings in Cape Town. It was built in 1679 by Dutch East India Company as a lodge for their slaves. The original building was one story with a courtyard that housed slaves as well as the criminals and the emotionally disturbed. In the mid 18th century the British acquired the building and added a second story. The slaves were moved to a different location and the British used it for government offices. Approximately 600 slaves were housed in this building at one time. In 1810 restoration took place and the lodge was used as the first post office, library, and Supreme Court in Cape Town.

Today the Slave Lodge is part of the South African Cultural History Museum where visitors can learn about Cape Town's history and view it's collections of South African ceramics, toys, tools, silver, textiles and view artifacts from ancient Egypt, Greece, and Rome and the near and far East."[83] (Ghana co.uk)

It is important to gain insight into what happened during the Slave trade from the enslaved Africans perspectives. The following account was a plea for mercy from an enslaved African at the Cape in South Africa. The severe punishments cast upon the Africans included intolerable beatings, branding, and parts of the body literally cut off. There was no anesthesia or pain medication administered, just butchery.

"Punishment at the Cape was severe, it is interesting that the Afrikaans word "soebat" meaning to plead, is from Malay origin. The slaves would have on many occasions used the word soebat. Runaway company slaves were whipped by a sjambok (Malay word, now part of the Afrikaans vocabulary) and branded on one cheek. With the next offence they were branded on the other cheek. Any further offence would lead to their nose and ears being cut off. Harsher punishment was dealt out for worse crimes. Punishment included; breaking on the wheel, pulling out flesh with red-hot tongs, mutilation, impaling, burning alive and slow strangulation. One slave woman who the authorities suspected of trying to strangle her child, the child died a week later, was to be punished by having her breast torn out by hot tongs. She was then to be burned to death, until there was only ashes. The authorities showed mercy and put her in a sack and drowned her in Table bay. The dead bodies of slaves were also left in public places as a warning to the rest of the slaves. When looking at the cruel punishment that was handed out to the slaves, the historical context should be taken into account. Burghers, who were punished, received nearly as gruesome forms of punishment as the slaves, from our present humanitarian position we find revolting."[84] (A.M. van Rensburg)

Bunce Island Slave Castle

"Bunce Island was one of about 40 slave castles, or fortified trading posts, that European merchants built along the coast of West Africa during the period of the Atlantic slave trade. Slave traders based at the castles purchased African captives, imprisoned them, and loaded them aboard the slave ships that took them on the infamous middle passage to America. Slave castles have been called "warehouses of humanity".

Bunce Island was also linked to the Northern Colonies. Slave ships from Rhode Island, Massachusetts, Connecticut; and New York frequently called at the castle, taking their human cargoes to the West Indies or back to the Southern Colonies. These Northern slave ships often purchased their African captives with rum produced in New England with molasses brought back to North America from the West Indies. While thousands of African

Americans are now visiting several famous West African slave castles each year especially Elmina Castle in Ghana and Goree Castle in Senegal – Bunce Island has a much more direct link to North America than these other historic sites. After visiting Bunce Island in 1991, Colin Powell said:

"I am an American…But today, I am something more…

I am an African too…I feel my roots here in this continent."[85] (BBC)

Slave Castles and Forts in the Central Region of Ghana

*Beraku Fort Good Hope

The Fort of Good Hope was built by the Dutch in 1667. It was taken over by the British in 1782, but regained by the Dutch through a treaty around 1785. The Fort was transferred back to the British in 1868. The Slaves were traded almost 150 years from 1745 forward. The fort held 50 to 100 Slaves at a time.

Food was dropped through a hole at the top of the men's dungeon to the floors below for the captives. They were fed like animals. Iron grates were placed at the bottom of the hole to make sure the Africans could not escape. The men closest to the hole ate, because there was never enough food for everyone. The hole provided the only light that the captives had. The dungeons were dark and filthy. A strong unpleasant order still fills the air.

The Hole in the Ceiling of the Men's Dungeon that Slavers used to throw Food to the Enslaved Africans

The door of no return has been sealed. The slaves were lead though a tunnel underground about two miles to Slave ships. As I looked through what was once the guard post peep holes, the coastal town was filled with the laughter of families and children swimming and fishing. This was not the case during the Slave trade. There was utter terror as the people surrounding the fishing village were kidnapped and other Africans were marched to the Fort from the interior villages.

The reoccurring thought that comes to mind is if I am visiting the area where my ancestors originated from prior to or during the Slave trade. But they are all of our ancestors, because as stated previously, we are all a part of Africa. This expedition is not getting easier it is progressively harder to take. My guide Daniel continues to remind me that I have a mission that must be completed for the good of others.

*Adam - Fort Leydsaemheyt - Fort Patience

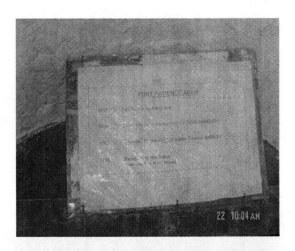

We visited the male dungeon first. The men were kept in chains either attached to the walls or to one another. Bats were hiding in the dungeon. There is no telling how many cases of rabies existed among enslaved Africans during the Slave trade. Up to 105 men were held captive in the small space. It would have been difficult for them to breath. The dungeon had no windows or holes for light or air. The stench is still unbearable. The men had to stoop down because the ceilings were too low. Daniel had to interpret what the guide was saying, because he was speaking in his native language. My picture was taken inside the female dungeon. There was a feeling of melancholy standing there. Once again I sensed the presence of the Ancestors.

The female dungeon held 104 women in a room chained to the walls and the floor. The chain that the Fort guide held had a spike shape at the end of it. The women were chained in such a way that they could not move. Women and girls were forced to wallow in their own urine, feces, and worse.

Spiked Chain used to confine Enslaved African Women and Door of No Return

The officers' quarters were upstairs. They brought the enslaved
African women and girls to their rooms and other places at the fort
and brutally raped them

From the male dungeons the men were lead out the door of
no return. We could hear the ocean behind the walls. On one
occasion the Slave traders dug a hole. They pushed some defiant
Africans into the hole, because they refused to go through the door

of no return. Eighty Nine Africans were buried alive.

I stood on the deck outside the officers' quarters with the view and sounds of the Atlantic Ocean roaring. I prayed at that moment that where ever this dissertation ends up that God will not allow the enslaved Africans' suffering to be taken for granted.

The fact finding mission to find the truth and pay respect to the pre-middle passage enslaved African history is progressing with a heavy heart. There are feelings of hurt, anger, and empathy. There is a continuous bombardment of information surfacing about millions of enslaved Africans. The majority with unknown names were tortured and murdered for power, greed, and inanimate objects.

Grave of Enslaved Africans Buried Alive for refusing to go
through the Door of no return

The world must understand that so many lives were lost and changed forever prior the middle passage. The church where the Slave traders worshipped and prayed was located on the top floor of the Fort. I wondered what they prayed for. Daniel commented that they probably prayed that none of the Slaves would die.

We saw ships in the near distance of the fort that gave a sense of what the ships may have looked like that many of the Africans, were carried away on. It took strength not to weep as long this time. The town around this castle is a poor area. There were cannons all around. The guide explained that the enslaved Africans who wanted to relieve themselves would have to stand in front of the cannon and beg the cannon not to fire on them. The cannons were strategically placed to keep the Africans from running away. The psychological mind games and torture the captures placed on the Africans was atrocious. The Africans were forced to build the Forts that held them captive. There is a school for small children located 100 feet from the fort. The towns were left in ruins by the Europeans.

*Abandze - Fort Amsterdam (Coromantine)

Chains that bound Africans, Door of No Return, Children from the
Village

     Fort Amsterdam was built in the sixteenth century and is
still standing. It was built without cement, only shells, sand,
ground shells, and palm oil. The fort was enlarged and improved
from 1681-82. The British took over temporarily in 1782 until the
Dutch regained control. The Asante conquered it and ransacked it
in 1806, and it was destroyed by Anomabus in 1811. Cannons
were all around the Fort because of its location and vulnerability
along the Atlantic Ocean. There was a ghastly appearance looming
over the fort from the street. It looked more like an abandoned
castle. There was a child carrying a tub on her head accompanied

by another child with food from the village for sell. They were standing on the winding staircase leading up to the fort. The fort tour guide explained how the original cooking tools were used by the enslaved African women to cook for the other Africans during the Slave trade. Africans marched sometimes hundreds of miles to Fort Amsterdam. I can't imagine the condition of their feet. There was also an interesting looking tree outside of what use to be the female dungeons. The leaves from it were used for upset stomach and other medicinal purposes.

The door of no return was not sealed. The male dungeons still contained the chains used to keep Africans attached to the wall. I stood in the door of no return that the enslaved Africans passed through to the waiting Slave ships.

Fort Guide, Door of no Return, Marlene standing in Door of no Return

The South West Bastion was labeled. We could hear the ocean in the background. The officers worshipped and prayed in the open area. The grounds surrounding Fort Amsterdam were filled with the graves of enslaved Africans and Slave traders. This

was also an ancestral burial ground. Many of the bodies of Africans were thrown into the ocean.

The Africans had no place to run. They were taken by canoe to the waiting Slave ships. The enslaved Africans were shipped from Fort Amsterdam to Australia, America, and Surinam. There was a thriving fishing village next to the fort.

*Anomabu Fort William Fort William

The Europeans first arrived at Fort William trading drunken wine and other items. The discovery of America and the Caribbean increased the need for Slaves to work in the tobacco and sugar cane fields. Slavery began here in 1514. There was a Slave auction room. The Slaves were weighed at this fort and sold according to their weight.

Marlene and Fort Guide at the Entrance and Courtyard

Most of the captives were sent to Jamaica and Barbados.
The heat was stifling that day in the Slave dungeon with the doors
open. It was probably unbearable for the enslaved Africans with

the doors closed.

Slave Dungeons, Auction Room/Dungeon, Path to Door of No Return

The Fantis' were the local people. I remarked to the guide that he looked a lot like my father's paternal side of the family, the Gary's. My brother's DNA proved the intuition to be true. The

Gary's have been traced to Ghana. Children were playing on the beach that carried Africans away from Africa on Slave ships.

Children play peaceably on the shores by the fort that once carried the local people away from Africa

Fort William – Cape Coast
This Fort William near Cape Coast Castle was built by the English in 1820 as a look out post and protector of Cape Coast Castle.

*Morié - Fort Nassau

Fort Nassau was built by the Dutch in 1612, and they enlarged it around 1620 as the demand for storing Slaves grew. It was enlarged again in the 1630's. The Fort was captured temporarily in the 1660's. The Dutch regained control in 1665 and Britain gained control in 1782. They agreed to return the fort to the Dutch because of a treaty agreement in 1785. When the British colonized Ghana, Britain regained control. The Fort is pretty much in ruins. I could see it from a distance. The roads were too bad leading up to the fort, so I took photographs of the Fort and the surrounding village.

* Fort SAO JORGE da MINA (Elmina) Castle

"In 1481, the Portuguese prince, Joao II, sent Diogo d'Azambuja (an experienced state official who had served the royal family in the past) to build a fortress at Elmina (Sao Jorge de Mina), the first and largest European building in the tropics."[86] (Adibe and Boateng)

Elmina Castle was built in 1482. The number of captives placed in each small dungeon was between 150 and 200. One of the male dungeons held 600 at a time. The normal enslavement at the castles and forts was 45 days to 3 months in most cases. Elmina's dominance of the Gold Coast trade lasted until 1637. The Dutch conquered Elmina Castle and maintained control almost 275 years. They increased the Slave trade. Elmina was enlarged using supplies shipped from Amsterdam. The Portuguese church in the courtyard was turned into a Slave market.

The Dutch refused to worship where the Portuguese Catholics worshipped previously, so they built a new chapel in another part of the castle. Elmina was located on the Gold coast.

"The incentives were various: the making of money, the 'saving' of Africans from 'barbarism', the excitement of voyages down the Guinea coast and of raiding expeditions up the rivers, the exertion of a febrile ingenuity in outwitting local African chiefs and middle-men as, on shipboard or within the dark stone chambers of Elmina, they haggled over the correct price to be paid for a Negro man, a Negro woman, or a Negro child."[87] (Hennessy 12)

I stood in front of the Governors quarters where the enslaved African women were brought from the dungeons below to be taken advantage of by the governor. Unfortunately there were some European women standing there laughing as the groups of Africans and I listened to the fort guide. It was so disrespectful. From the governors' bedroom we could see the entire castle. The church and dungeons were also in view.

Female Dungeon

Staircase to Governor's Quarters

Deck of Governors' Quarters

There was a chapel where the Slave traders prayed and held church service above the dungeons. The Dutch used the Church as a market hall.

Entrance to the Chapel

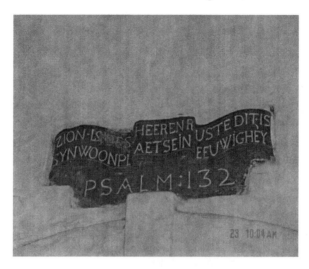

Governor's Quarters

We walked through the male dungeon to a tunnel that was completely dark. The smell and sense of the painful Slave misery was noticeable. The floors in the dungeons were made of stone. The captives were packed in like sardines. We won't speak of the rodents that ran rampant through out the castle while it was used to house Slaves. The source of light and ventilation was close to zero. There was a trench that went from the castle to the ocean towards the west for the human waste and no telling what else. The captives slept with their urine and feces all night.

The Africans were given boiled yams to eat. There was a struggle for the food. If the captives tried to fight for their rights, they were tortured or put in the condemned cell to die. The condemned dungeons at Elminia and other Slave sites were really death chambers for the difficult Africans. Once a person was sentenced to those dungeons, they did not come out alive. The bodies sometimes rotted and decomposed beyond recognition. At most of the castles and forts the dead bodies were either thrown to the wind in the surrounding jungles, or put in the Atlantic Ocean for the sharks to feed on.

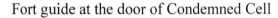

Fort guide at the door of Condemned Cell

Entrance to Condemned Cell

Descendant of Enslaved African Ancestors from Sierra Leone,
Liberia, and Ghana Africa at the Door of No Return

*Fort St. Jago in Elmina
Elmina - Fort St. Jago (Cobnraadsburg)

Fort St. Jago is within walking distance of Elmina Castle.
The Dutch controlled fort made Elmina Castle an easy target. The
Dutch finally conquered Elmina after three tries. Fort St. Jago was
used to protect Elmina Castle militarily, because they were both
controlled by the Dutch. Slaves were not housed there. It also
served as a prison for Europeans.

*Cape Coast Castle
The British owned Cape Coast Castle

    The castle was built by the British Royal African Company Adventures. The Dutch fought the Danes, they fought the Swedish, and they fought the Portuguese because of the strategic location of the land along the Atlantic coast. The Portuguese were credited as the first to land on the shore. They supposedly came to Christianize the Ghanaians, and to teach them Gospel reasons for Christ according to our guide. This killed the traditional Islamic teachings. The Portuguese were to live and stay in Elmina. Africans were exchanged for slat. The Europeans named it Ivory Coast because the Slaves came from Benin. It was also called the Slave Coast. The castles and first forts were built for the Europeans to get the gold and water. Then the Europeans began fighting each other for control of the castles. The cannons were facing the ocean to protect the fort from attack. The British were competing with the Dutch and vise versa. The same type of competition existed between the Portuguese and the Dutch. Europeans came to trade Gold, thereby naming this area the Gold Coast. They told the Chiefs they needed people with skin that could easily be identified to build the newly discovered lands of the Americas and Caribbean. Yesterday we visited Fort William and now the other Fort William is in view from Cape Coast Castle. There is no way that the Europeans can deny the role they played in the Slave trade. Liverpool sent representatives that would differentiate the slaves for each owner. They would brand the Africans with the branding of the company that purchased them. Africans were sent from Kumasi to Cape Coast Castle. The Slaves were shipped to Jamaica, Trinidad, and South Carolina for work in the sugarcane and tobacco fields. Enslaved Africans were also shipped to England for construction.

My Ghanaian guide Daniel and I entered the museum first. There were replicas and actual artifacts from Slave ships. Original ropes and chains from the Slave ships have been preserved. I held in my hand a rope that held enslaved Africans while they were helplessly chained, tied, and bound together in the bottom of Slave ships. There was a diagram of the way the Africans were stacked and packed on the slave ships.

Posters advertising African Slaves for rent or for sale at Auction

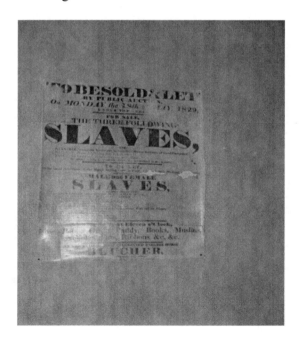

Morgan Mason was the fort guide. We entered the male slave dungeons first. There was a tunnel between the male and female dungeons

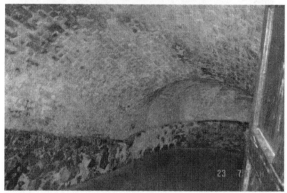

The female dungeons were close to the governors' quarters. There was very little light and no ventilation. It was hot and sticky. The two sections for the female Slaves held 150 to 200 in each section. The women and girls did not bath the entire time they were there unless they were chosen to be taken advantage of sexually by the male Slave traders or governors.

Female Slave Dungeons

The Europeans changed the names of the Africans during the Slave trade. The locals still use the European names. Many Africans in the towns surrounding the castle have the common name Professor and a given family name that they are called by other locals in the community. Our fort guide's European name is Ed Robert Morgan Mason. Manson's Fanti' given name is Aswoud.

Buried in the courtyard of the Cape Coast Castle are two Europeans and a Slave. Major McClain, his wife and a Slave. McClain's father was Minister of the house. McClain was educated in England and came back to Africa and remained at Cape Coast Caste until his death. He died of malaria. His wife spent two month in mourning and killed herself because her husband had an enslaved African mistress named Ellen.

The Governors' quarters were on the top floor. Most of the governors of the castle died of malaria and were buried in the Dutch cemetery. Some of officers stood on the officers' quarter steps. They would move the men and women to the courtyard and choose the women they wanted to rape. Some of the enslaved African women became their permanent girlfriends. The ones that were impregnated by the Europeans were treated better than the other Slaves. Unknown numbers of enslaved Africans took their own lives. Others were sentenced to the condemned cells that were really death chambers for the obstinate and disobedient Africans. Once a person was sentenced to those dungeons, they were forced to stay in the cell until everyone in there died. So depending on how long it took to die, they were tortured by staying with stinking dead rotting bodies. No food or water was allowed. With the sweltering heat, the enslaved African's suffering was unimaginable. They were in the dark recesses of hell on earth. Once it was verified that everyone was dead, their bodies were not buried but thrown into the Atlantic Ocean or the jungles that once surrounded the castle.

The enslaved Africans were shackled one to another and were not given food or water once they entered the condemned cell. Some individuals from our tour group went in the condemned cell and came right back out. There was the horrible smell of death in that cell hundreds of years later. The smell made some of us sick to our stomachs.

Marlene and Mason in front of a Dungeon

Hole in the Ceiling used to drop food to Captives in the Dungeon

We visited the church that was located on the second floor over the dungeons. It was also used to market and negotiate the sale of enslaved Africans. There were maps and photographs on the walls. Two other churches were in view in the near distance. The Portuguese first used Christianity to enslave the Africans. What was once the Chapel at the Castle has been turned into a library for children.

The officers could see all of the dungeons from the second floor. We could see Cape Coast - Fort William in the near distance. The Dutch would send messages to the other castles and forts they controlled. In the Palva hall, the auctioning of Slaves began as soon as the Slave traders entered the hall, because there was always confusion. The traders usually did not agree on the prices asked for the Africans. The authorities had to listen to the merchants. The Slave traders examined the Slaves' entire bodies. This was done very disrespectfully. The men and women were displayed naked.

Slaves were kept at Elmina Castle, Cape Coast, Antonio, and Jago. The Dutch Fort William on the cape coast and Victory were for security. They did not hold Slaves. Over 35 forts were built. In Accra some of the forts cannot be traced and no traces of them remain, while others are in fair to good shape considering there age. The local chiefs say they should be forgiven for marginalizing other tribes as inferior. The Ghanaians sold the Nigerians. They battled each other and they sold Africans for the Dutch in Amsterdam from the Volta region. The enslaved Africans were considered ignorant and less than human. Morgan Mason commented that "we cannot still be doing the blaming game. It already happened. We should forget about the past and forge ahead. It takes two to forgive. Now they are for Christ, and we can't keep blaming. Our duty is to plan and forge ahead and develop better relationships."

Buyers and sellers and demand for supplies of Slaves were the focus of the castle. The tunnel could be seen from the platform that led to the door of no return. The tunnel could also be seen from the Slave dungeons. We stepped down into the female dungeon. I could not stay in the dungeon. I had an eerie feeling and stepped out. During Slavery, the men walked through a tunnel to join the female slaves with their backs bent to go through the door of no return. The captives passed through the door of no return one at a time in groups of five.

Morgan demonstrates required posture of
Africans passing through the Door of No Return

Path Africans walked to Slave ships

Our group passed through the door of no return to view what the enslaved Africans saw on their last walk to the Slave ships that carried them away from Africa forever. Ships were in view in the distance of the fishing villages near the castle. There was a somber sense of what the Ancestors may have felt waiting to be loaded onto the Slave ships. We passed back through the Door of Return into the castle. For many of us, it was a right of passage home to Africa in honor of all the enslaved African ancestors. It is hard to explain, but there was a sense of peace walking back through the Door of Return.

"Door of Return"

We watched the keeper of the shrine perform rituals to the departed ancestors in the traditional African manner. He sent good will messages to the Ancestors. Nana respect meant wishing the ancestors the best so they could pass safely in peace. He said, "To all mighty God, over everything, from the shine to the departed ancestors, please grant peace." Reefs placed by African Americans and other enslaved African descendants throughout the Diaspora aligned the walls of the shrine. The reefs where placed to respect the enslaved Africans that passed through the castle or died there. Some descendants return to the castle every year. They wished rest for our ancestors and that they may all rest in peace.

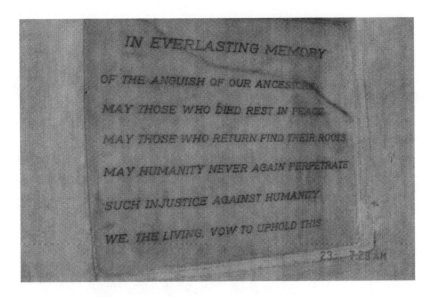

IN EVERLASTING MEMORY

OF THE ANGUISH OF OUR ANCESTORS

MAY THOSE WHO DIED REST IN PEACE

MAY THOSE WHO RETURN FIND THEIR ROOTS

MAY HUMANITY NEVER AGAIN PERPETRATE

SUCH INJUSTICE AGAINST HUMANITY

WE, THE LIVING, VOW TO UPHOLD THIS

Western Region

*Shama Fort St. Sebastian

I attended a wonderful Ghanaian church service that morning with one of the waitresses at the hotel where I was staying. My next commission was to visit more Slave dungeons in search of the truth. After traveling a good distance to find out upon arrival that fort St. Sebastian was closed for repairs was disappointing. But, as God would have it, the fort Guide was gracious enough to conduct a tour of the fort. The Portuguese built this wooden fort in 1558. In 1637 the Dutch occupied it. In 1664 the English captured it. In 1665 the Dutch regained possession of it and rebuilt it. In 1872, the fort was ceded to the British.

The fort was painted and whitewashed on the outside. The truth was waiting inside. This time, I saw actual bones from enslaved Africans, the elbow, shin, and more.

I held in my hand a chain that once held enslaved African women and children against their will. The fort guide held the one for men.

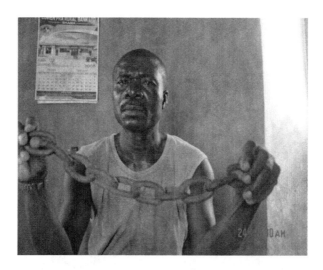

There was another condemned cell. At this fort, men, boys, women, and girls were raped. According to the fort guide, from 1000 to 2500 captives were crammed into dungeons at St. Sebastian at one time. The captives stayed up to three months or more waiting for the next Slave ship.

The Slaves were chained together and lowered through a hole to an underground tunnel below leading to awaiting Slave ships. The area where the Slave ships once docked is marked with a cross.

*Dixcove – Fort Metal Cross

The fort was on the bay called "Dick's or Dickies Cove".
The work to build this British fort was initiated by the British

Royal African Company in 1692 and completed in 1698 due to attacks from the Ahanta people, and continuous disputes between the English and the Brandenburgers. The fort is believed to be on the same site of an earlier post. The fort was besieged from 1748-56 and abandoned in 1826. It was re-occupied in 1830. It was transferred to the Dutch and renamed Metalen Kruis, in 1868. The Dutch gave it over to Britain in 1872. It came under Dutch control in 1867 and later reverted to the British in 1872. The British restored the fort from 1954-56. This British fort has been white washed and painted in recent years.

During the British era, the fort served as the District officer's residence and administrative offices, state council, police and post office. It is currently leased to the African Gateway (Ghana) Limited, to sympathetically improve and adapt it for use as a restaurant in part, and as accommodations for visitors and staff. It is currently being used as a lodge. Because the English was directly involved with Slavery in the United States along with the Portuguese, there is anger over this fort being painted and whitewashed to be used and viewed in a more humane way. The door of no return has been sealed. I was able to ring the bell in the tower. For me to ring the bell meant that I was ringing a bell of freedom in honor of all of the enslaved ancestors that were enslaved at the fort, and passed through the Door of No Return to the oceans and lands of their deaths.

Female Slave Dungeon, Slave Courtyard

*Fort St. Antonio in Axim
AXIM - Fort San Antonio, Fort Santo Antonio de Axim (Axim)

Slavery and Christianity the Untold Story   133

Henry Currant was the guide at Fort St. Antonio. St. Antonio is located in Axim, and it is the second oldest fort in Ghana. This fort was also built by the Portuguese along with Elmina Castle. The name Axim was derived from miscommunication between a villager and the Portuguese. When the Portuguese arrived, the local people had never seen a white man. One of women from the village got away, but the woman who was caught was asked by the Portuguese what the area was called. She said "Axim", which means do you know me? The woman was asking the Portuguese if they knew her. The Portuguese thought she was telling them the name of the area. So the area became know as Axim. The Portuguese were the first to arrive on the coast of Ghana. They originally went to Shama, but the trading was not successful, so they shifted to Elimina in 1471.

The Portuguese split into two groups, one at Elmina, and the other in Axim in 1502. They began building the fort in 1503, and in 1515 it was completed. The Portuguese named the fort St. Antonio. They traded mango, ivory, and cola nuts with the natives from the surrounding villages. The Portuguese received word from America that there was a lot of tobacco and sugarcane there. The majority of the enslaved Africans were shipped to America from this location. By the end of the 16th century the Portuguese started the Slave trade. When the Slave trade began, many of the families from the surrounding villages traded their wives, children, other family members, and friends with the Portuguese for salt, tobacco, rum, sugar, and other items. There were four dungeons with an overwhelming stench in each one.

The captives were held at the Fort up to three months waiting to be shipped to America. The Portuguese preferred children, because they could work before they were grown. Children normally lived longer than adults, so the profits were higher. There were two women's dungeons. They kept the women separated that the slave traders sexually abused. The women's dungeons were small. The dungeon for the beautiful women held up to twenty four captives at a time. This room also had two chairs for sitting, and four tiny windows at the top for air and light. The other dungeons had almost no air and very little to no light. There was a rock and a ledge for the women to sit on. This rock was for the most beautiful women. The Slave master took his pick of women to take sexual advantage of. The food was put on the floors for all of the captives. The women ate, slept, and defecated on that floor. It is no wonder that the smells were still very strong almost 500 years later. The women and other slaves were auctioned for sale in the dungeon with the rock. When a price was agreed upon, the governor of the fort hit a piece of steel with a hammer. The enslaved Africans were branded with hot irons. Then they were shoved through the door of no return and sent through tunnels to the waiting Slave ships bound for America most of the time.

Africans were also kidnapped and forced through the door of no return pictured below. Their unsuspecting families thought they were working at the fort as laborers in exchange for goods. This door was so high off the ground that when the Africans jumped down, there was no way for them to climb back up. Some of them jumped to their deaths or were badly injured. Now mind you they were chained one to another, so they had to drag the dead and injured through the tunnel and out to the Slave ship. Most of the captives from Fort Antonio were shipped to America. The first shipment of enslaved Africans consisted of 120 with only 14 surviving the journey.

Door of No Return that lead to a long Underground Tunnel to awaiting Slave Ships

The Portuguese were poor when they arrived in Africa. The Slave trade provided their wealth. The Dutch knew the Portuguese were making a lot of money, so they captured the fort in 1642. The Portuguese were at St. Antonio for 120 years. The Dutch were at the Fort for 230 years. In 1807 the abolitionist British Lawyers William Wilberforce and David Livingston arrived to set the Slaves free. Some of the enslaved Africans were taken to Sierra Leone and Liberia and set free. The strongest Africans shouted that "they got free from them". The Dutch tried to destroy the fort, and in 1872 the British bought the fort from the Dutch. They were exporting gold to the United States. The grave of the Dutch captain William Boxford is at the fort. The story told was that he saw the beautiful African women and fell backward off the deck and broke his neck in 1703. The sun dial clock was first placed at the front of the fort. Then it was moved to the Slave courtyard. When it was time for the Slave master and soldiers to go for their meals, they placed a gun in front of the clock. They brought all of the Africans to sit in the courtyard. The mental brain washing that took place was appalling. The Dutch would tell the Africans that if they moved the gun would shot them. So the captives would sit still in fear of the gun shooting them. But if they needed to relieved themselves, they would ask the gun not to shoot them. They would say to the gun, "I'll be right back, and I just need to relieve myself and promise to return" for example.

Portrait of Captain Boxford

*Fort Appolonia in Beyin off Ekwe

Entrance

Guide in front of Male Dungeons

This British fort was built between 1750 and 1770. There was a business office at the entrance where the price and items were negotiated for the enslaved Africans. This fort was built later than the others in comparison. There was a back staircase leading from the governor's quarters to the female dungeon. Seeing the bed in the female dungeon sent chills down my spine. The Fort was partially reconstructed in the 1960s to use it as a lodge.

Governor's Quarters, Staircase to Female Dungeon, Female Dungeon

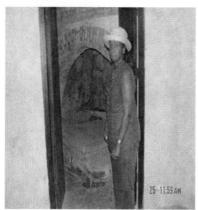

Fort Christianborg

Fort Christianborg was originally built in 1525 by the Swedes as a lodge not a fort. They controlled it until 1660 when the Dutch took it from the Swedes. In 1661 the Danes captured it and made it into a fort. It was renamed Fort Christianborg. The Danes occupied Fort Christianborg for almost 200 years. The Danish governor sold it to the Portuguese for a short time. The Portuguese renamed it Fort Sao Francisco Xavier. They abandoned the fort in

1682. In 1683 it was occupied by the Akwamu tribe until the Danish took it over. Fort Fredrichsburg occupied it in 1683. They moved their headquarters from Fort Fredrichsburg to Fort Christianborg in 1685. The Danes regained control in 1694. They sold it to the British in 1850. The Fort became the official residence of Dr. Kwame Nkrumah, First President of Ghana in 1960 and has remained as the Seat of Government. It was frequently rebuilt with additions in recent years, and the Fort is currently not open to the public. A new government building was under construction while I was there. It may become a museum when the new building is completed.

Princesstown - Groot-Friedrichsburg or Fort Hollandia

It was a Danish lodge in 1658. It was enlarged and turned into a fort in 1682. The Fort was abandoned in 1716. John Conny, a local chief stayed there in 1717. He stayed until 1725 when the Dutch conquered the fort and renamed it Fort Hollandia. The Dutch maintained control until the British captured it in 1872.

Takrama-Fort Sophie Louise

The Lodge was built by the Brandenburgers in 1690.

Britain captured the fort in 1691. The fort was abandoned in 1708. The British sold it to the Dutch in 1717.

Akwida - Fort Dorothea

Fort Dorothea was built by the Brandenburgers, in 1685. The Dutch controlled it from 1687-90. They gave the fort back to the Brandenburgers, in 1698. Fort Dorothea was abandoned about 1709. The Dutch took it back in 1712 and relinquished it back to the Brandenburgers in 1712. The Dutch sold the Fort in 1718.

Butri - Fort Batensteyn

Fort Batensteyn was built by the Swedish as a trading post from 1650-52. The Dutch turned it into a fort in 1656. The English fought against the Dutch and took the Fort 1665. It was abandoned in 1818-27. The Dutch rebuilt it in 1828, and relinquished the Fort by treaty and the Fort remained under Dutch control until 1872, when it was transferred to the British.

Praso Castle

The Praso Castle was near what is now the Assin Praso Heritage village and mass grave site. There is only a commemorative marking where the castle once stood. The Dutch grew inpatient with burying individual enslaved Africans, so they literally dumped the enslaved African bodies into a mass grave.

Sekondi - Fort Orange

Fort Orange was built by the Dutch and dates back around

1640. It started as a lodge and was turned into a fort in 1740. The fort was turned over to Britain in 1872 with the colonization of Ghana. The fort has served as a light house since 1872.

*Kumasi Asanti Region

I met with Mr. Osei Kwadwo, the curator and writer/author of Ashanti History.

Marlene and Asante Historian, Asirifi Danquah, and Asanti Royal family executive Staff

Salaga Slave Market

Most enslaved African descendants visit Elmina and Cape Coast castle because of their popularity as tourist sites and proximity to Accra. But few have an opportunity to visit an area in Central Ghana where Africans were sold and received their last baths prior to marching on to Slave castles and forts along the Cape Coast of Ghana. Many of the Slaves were auctioned in neighboring countries to Ghana like Burkina Faso and were forced to walk to Salaga to be auctioned to the highest bidders. There were no shores in Ghana at that time. Anyone who was captured in Burkina Faso and the Volta region were forced to walk to Salaga and other Slave markets. Some Africans hid in Slave caves to avoid the traps of Slave traders. The Slave caves were located near Techiman Ghana.

Salaga was a major Slave market within 100 miles of the Cape Coast Slave castles and forts. The murals were located on the grounds of the old Slave market. Some murals portrayed what the enslaved Africans endured at the Slave markets and Slave Rivers. Others were of abolitionist, freedom fighters, and civil rights leaders.

Murals of abolitionists and Civil Rights Leaders

"Others were captured from the neighboring African states like Cote d'Ivoire, Burkina Faso, Togo, the southern part of Nigeria, the Gambia, Mali and Senegal. Later, the British went to Angola and Congo to buy some Captives. Some selective slave markets in the then Gold Coast were at Wa, Salaga, Yendi, Paga, Sandema, Tamale, Yeji, Techiman, Abonsi, Ningo, Assin, Fosu, and Assin Manso. Generally, the European Merchants did not travel further inland for captives. They rather depended upon the middle men who bought them from some traditional rulers and some trade dealers like Samori and Babatu." [86] (Ghana Ministry of Tourism 28)

"Donko Nsuo", Slave River

Enslaved Africans were sometimes forced to travel hundreds of miles to the Donko Nsuo Slave River. When they reached the river, they were chained to trees while waiting to be bathed. They were humiliated and totally disrespected. The slave traders washed the men and the women. They put shea butter on the captives to make them appear to be in better physical condition to get a better price at the Slave Market.

Marlene at the Entrance of the Slave River

Once again the chains I heard breaking in the vision experience during the prophetic prayer described in Chapter II was of great significance as I hesitated to enter the door to the Slave River.

"Donko Nsuo in Assin Manso in the Central Region is less

than hundred kilometers from where the slave ships docked at Cape Coast and Elmina, and this is where the captives were encamped for their last bath with African water, in a river know as "Donko Nsuo", Slave River."[87] (Ghana Ministry of Tourism 18)

Marlene Overcome with Emotion as the Guide Describes Horrifying Experiences of Enslaved Africans at the Slave Rivers

Slave Murals at the Assin Manso Historic Slave Site

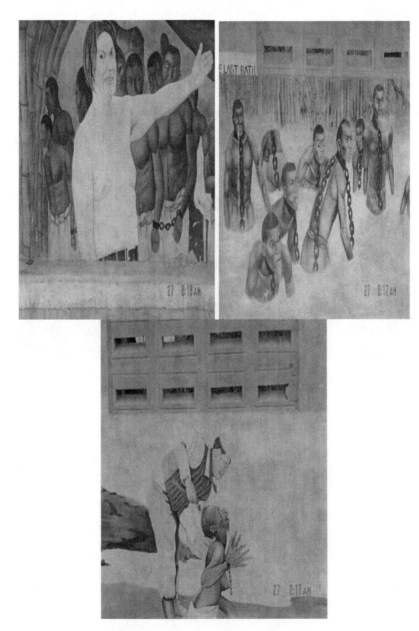

Ghanaian Guide Daniel walks to Slave River

"The captives were marched down to the Coast from the countryside and along the Coastal areas through bush paths. They walked through the scorching sun barefooted. Traveling was always difficult and impossible during the rainy season. They could be attacked by some wild animals like lions, elephants and leopards; bitten by snakes; swallowed by crocodiles; stung by swarm of bees and scorpions and sucked by tsetse fly. They might have been suffered from such tropical diseases like malaria, yellow fever, yaws and guinea worm. They waded through big rivers. Some mothers carried their babies on their backs. Stubborn captives were flogged or whipped and some were maimed. Some look pale and wore on tattered clothes.

There is a tree stump on the left entrance which has a lot of secrets about the slave trade, who were being captured and chained to it either after bathing or before. The Slave Trade, in which Africans were forcibly taken from their homes in the 16th century and thereafter, and sent to the Americas to work as slaves, stands condemned for all time.

As the human part of the "triangular trade", our ancestors were hunted, captured and treated as merchandise. From the place and time they were captured, it was the march of no return from the Salaga Slave market where the sorting out and initial changing of hands took place. In those days, there were no cargo trains, no airfreight services, and no cattle trucks. They marched to the coast in an arduous, demeaning and dangerous journey. Chained and manacled, with stock around their necks, the greatest abuse of human rights in history was enacted for real. Faced with hunger and disease, cruelty of slave raiders and other dangers of the hazardous journey took their toll on the way. Many bodies were strewn along this path, left for dead, killed for their defiance, their bodies left for vultures and hyenas to feed upon." [89] (Ghana Ministry of Tourism 18)

Slave Market Murals

Assin Praso Heritage Village and the Slave Crossing Point

Mass Grave

Nnonokosie' Mass Grave for the enslaved Africans who died, or were murdered near the Slave River 'Nnonkonsuo' where the enslaved Africans received their Last Baths

After the enslaved Africans were sold at the Slave Markets and received their last baths in the Slave River, they were chained together and marched to the Slave Castles and Forts on the Cape Coast of Ghana.

Endnotes:

(81) John 8:32

(82) Breaking the Silence www.antislavery.org - Ghana.co.uk - 1999-2001

(83) The Slave Lodge - Ghana.co.uk - 1999-2001

(84) My Genetic Enrichment, Slaves at the Cape, South Africa - A.M. van Rensburg

(85) BBC.co.uk 1/22/07

(86) Portugal, the Mother of all Slavers Part 1 New African - Patrick Adibe and Osei Boateng - March 2000 Issue - (Page 24)

(87) The Atlantic Slave Traders 1441-1807 James Pope-Hennessy - Castle Books - 1967 – (Page 12)

(88) Joseph Project Souvenir Book - Ghana Ministry of Tourism 2007- (Page 18)

(89) Joseph Project Souvenir Book - Ghana Ministry of Tourism 2007 - (Page 18)

CHAPTER V – RESULTS OF THE RESEARCH

The Middle Passage

The Europeans originally came to West Africa for trade starting with the Portuguese and the Dutch. The need for laborers in the Americas and Caribbean to work with sugarcane and tobacco, and the profits derived from the Slave trade propelled the enslavement of the African people to another level. The fact that most of the Africans had never seen a white man gave the Europeans an unfair advantage over the Africans. The ships for trade were modified to pack as many of the enslaved human cargo for shipment as possible. The Europeans kidnapped and took by force anyone and anything they wanted. In the previous chapters the purpose and people responsible for the Slave trade were detailed. The Slave castles and forts were the processing centers, and the middle passage was for the payoff.

The middle passage was the mode of transport used to deliver the goods and the precious cargo of Slave labor previously ordered to the purchasers and would be purchasers at the different destinations known as the middle passage or triangular route. Some may wonder why the precious enslaved African people were referred to as, cargo. The Africans were considered as cargo by the heartless ship captains and crews and Slave traders and owners. The Slave ships were used to steal families away from everyone and everything they knew or held dear in Africa.

"The Trans-Atlantic Slave Trade resulted in the forced movement of men and women particularly between ages fifteen and thirty five who were tragically uprooted and inhumanly transported from the motherland. They were extracted from their paths of development, separated from their kith and kin and transplanted to foreign lands under a system of Slavery." [90] (Ghana Ministry of Tourism 3)

Many of the Slaves were sold or resold once the Ships docked at there appointed destinations. The ships were reloaded with the goods from the Caribbean, the West Indian Islands, and the Americas. Goods like tobacco, sugar, rum, guns, and resold Slaves were loaded onto the same Slave ship for the next destination. Europe was the final leg of the Slave ship voyage. The ship docked and the same process started all over again.

"Once in the Americas, sailors off-loaded those Africans who had survived the journey and sold them in the markets in the Americas where the captives began their life of labor as slaves. The ships then returned to Europe with goods produced by the subsequent slave labor. With this triangular trade, European capital, African labor, and American land and resources combined to supply an emerging global economy." [91](Mariners Museum)

The Africans were shipped as cargo, and they were counted in the ships records with the other goods. The enslaved Africans had no idea what was awaiting them on the stormy waters of the Atlantic Ocean and Mediterranean seas. The majority of them were branded with the initials of their new owners. Their freshly burned skin from the hot branding irons had not healed prior to their voyages. The horrifying and inhumane reality of the middle passage of the Slave trade is described in this chapter. Accounts of incidents and uprisings on the Slave ships and photographs of records obtained from the Maritime museums in Europe are included.

The Slave traders praised God for mercy in capturing Slaves and their success at fort Christianborg in 1733. There was no remorse for the 199 lives or additional African lives lost out of the 443.

"God be praised for his mercy in the preceding year; may He still assist us! In the name of Jesus we began the year 1733. On the 9th of January, Captain Hammer came onboard sick from Cabo Cortso. On the 14th of January we anchored at the fort Christianborg; God be praised for a good journey; may He still help. Our Captain died at the fort 2 hours after he was brought there. His successor is the Chief Officer Jaeger. On the 5th of February, 44 Slaves were delivered to us from the fort; all had been branded on the same thigh with the letters CB. On the 21st of February the governor came on board with letters, documents and eight Slaves with the brand CB on the one thigh. In the beginning on March we left Guinea after we had got 443 Slaves in all. At the time of departure, 90 had died. On the 7th of May we arrived at St. Thomas, thanks be to God for his mercy. We then had only 242 Slaves on board. 199 were dead, and two had been sold at the Coast of Guinea. From the 7th of March, a Slave died every day, which damage God then righted with a good crossing. The price for the living balanced the loss from the dead. On the 8th of May we delivered the first 27 good items with the brand CB. One week later the auction could start." [92] (Hansen 14)

The amount of time the ships took to bring products for trade to Africa and return to Europe, the Americas, and the Caribbean with human cargo and other goods averaged 60 to 90 days. The demand for Slaves was so great that larger Slave ships were built and others were modified to keep up with the demand and profits potential. The Slave ship captains and crews packed as many Africans on the ships as possible because their survival rate was very low. Lives lost meant nothing, because Slave captures, traders and owners may have viewed Africans as crop right for the pickings in all seasons.

"The time a ship took to make the Middle Passage depended upon several factors including its point of origin in Africa, the destination in the Americas, and conditions at sea such as winds, currents, and storms. With good conditions and few delays, a 17th-century Portuguese slave ship typically took 30 to 50 days to sail from Angola to Brazil. British, French, and Dutch ships transporting slaves between Guinea and their Caribbean island possessions took 60 to 90 days. A century or so later, larger merchant ships came into use in the trade and reduced these times somewhat." [93] (Mariners' Museum)

There were many Slaving ports throughout Europe and the Americas during the Slave trade. For the French, Nantes was the major slaving port. Liverpool and London were major Slaving ports for the British; Amsterdam for the Dutch, and Madrid for Spain. The Slaving ports for the Americas were intertwined with Europe, because many countries in Europe controlled the land in

America during most of the Slave trade. The major Slaving ports in the Americas included North and South Carolina in the south and New Amsterdam and other New England territories in the North, because of there strategic locations on the coast of the Atlantic Ocean.

"In 1594 the ship L'Espérance (meaning 'hope') which was registered at this port, became the first French ship to be identified as participating in the slave trade. By the late 18th Century slavers made up a full third of the traffic which passed between the medieval towers of the Old Port.

Nantes, on the Atlantic coast of France was the country's major slaving port, with over 1,400 voyages leaving for Africa during the 18th Century, 357 of them belonging to a single trading family, the Montaudoins. In 1754 the ship Saint-Phillipe, owned by the Nantes based Jogue brothers crossed the middle passage with 462 slaves in 25 days, whereas vessels earlier in the century would often take up to nine months. Nantes remained the principal slave port until the 1780s. Even after the official end of the slave trade in 1818, the trade continued. Over the next 13 years, 305 expeditions are recorded as having left from Nantes docks for the African coast. [94](Mariners Museum)

In order to present a realistic picture of what happened to millions of enslaved Africans during the middle passage journeys, the following paragraphs will provide details about the enslaved Africans' experiences. The information provides a window into the rapes on board slaving ships, the lives lost, murders, deaths, suicides, and insurrections by Slaves. The revolts detail the Slaves attempts to survive the hell they were in on the ships and would face when they landed. One of the most disturbing facts was the presence of a priest, a minister, and or missionaries on many of the Slave ships who did nothing to stop the murders and abuses that took place on the voyages.

"The man came aboard the slave ship Brooks in late 1783 or early 1784 with his entire family-his wife, two daughters, and mother-all convicted of witchcraft. The man had been a trader, perhaps in slaves; he was from a village called Saltpan, on the

Gold Coast. He was probably Fante. He knew English, and even though he apparently disdained to talk to the captain, he spoke to members of the crew and explained how he came to be enslaved. He had quarreled with the village chief, or "caboceer," who took revenge by accusing him of witchcraft, getting him and his family convicted and sold to the ship. They were now bound for Kingston, Jamaica.

When the family came on board, noted the physician of the ship, Thomas Trotter, the man "had every symptom of a sullen melancholy." He was sad, depressed, in shock. The rest of the family exhibited "every sign of affliction." Despondency, despair, and even "torpid insensibility" were common among the enslaved when they first came aboard the slave ship. The crew would have expected the spirits of the man and his family to improve as time passed and the strange new wooden world great more familiar.

The man immediately refused all sustenance. From the beginning of his captivity aboard the ship, he simply would not eat. This reason, too, was commonplace, but he went further. Early one morning, when sailors went below to check on the captives, they found the man a bloody mess. They urgently called the doctor. The man had attended to cut his own throat wound and apparently considered force-feeding the man. The throat wound, however, "put it out of our power to use any compulsory means," which were of course common on slavers. He referred to the speculum oris, the long, thin mechanical contraption used to force open unwilling throats to receive gruel and hence sustenance.

The following night the man made a second attempt on his own life. He tore out the sutures and cut his throat on the other side. Summoned to handle a new emergency, Trotter was cleaning up the bloody wound when the man began to talk to him. He declared simply and straightforwardly that "he would never go with white men." He then "looked wistfully at the skies" and uttered several sentences Trotter could not understand. He had decided for death over slavery.

The young doctor tended to him as best he could and ordered a "diligent search" of the apartment of the enslaved men for the instrument he had used to cut his throat. The sailors found nothing. Looking more closely at the man and finding blood on his fingertips and "ragged edges" around the wound, Trotter concluded that he had ripped open his throat with his own fingernails.

Yet the man survived. His hands were secured to "prevent any further attempt," but all the efforts came to naught against the will of the nameless man. Trotter later explained that "he still however adhered to his resolution, refused all sustenance, and died about a week or ten days afterwards of mere want of food."[95] (Rediker 17-18)

The following is an account of an unnamed woman referred to as "The Boatswain" because of her ability to keep order. Her intention as a peace maker was to keep as many of the enslaved Africans alive as possible. But she never made it out of the middle passage.

"The Boatswain"

Leadership among the captives arose from below deck during the Middle Passage. A sailor aboard the Nightingale told the story of a captive woman whose real name is lost to posterity but who came to be known on board the ship as "the boatswain" because she kept order among her fellow enslaved women, probably with a fierce determination that they should all survive the ordeal of oceanic crossing. She "used to keep them quiet when in the rooms, and when they were on deck likewise.

One day in early 1769, her own self-constituted authority clashed with that of the ship's officers. She "disobliged" the second mate, who gave her "a cut or two" with a cat-o'-nine-tails. She flew into a rage at this treatment and fought back, attacking the mate. He in turned pushed her away and lashed her smartly three or four more times. Finding herself, overmatched added frustrated that she could not "have her revenge of hem," she instantly "sprung two or three feet on the deck, and dropped down dead." Her body was thrown overboard about half an hour later, and torn to pieces by sharks."[96] (Rediker 16)

It was important for the enslaved Africans that did survive the middle passage journey to continue some of the traditions from their homeland. Food, dance, songs, and other customs were retained most times in secret. The enslaved African given the name Sarah by the Slave ship captain was one of the few to survive a Slave ship revolt and pass on some of the African traditions.

"When the young woman came aboard the Liverpool slave ship the Hudibrus in Old Calabar in 1785, she instantly captured everyone's attention. She had beauty, grace , and charisma: "Sprightliness was in her every gesture, and good nature beamed in her eyes. When the African musicians and instruments came out on the main deck twice a day for "dancing," the exercising of the enslaved, she "appeared to great advantage, as she bounded over the quarter-deck. To rude strains of African melody," observed a smitten sailor named William Butterworth. She was the best dancer and the best singer on the ship. "Ever lively! Ever gay!" seemed to sum up her aura, even under the extreme pressure of enslavement and exile.[5]

Other sailors joined Butterworth in admiration, and indeed so did Captain Jenkin Evans, who selected this young woman and one other as his "favourites," to whom he therefore "showed greater favours than the rest," likely as small recompense for coerced sexual service. Slave ship sailors like Butterworth usually detested the captain's favorites, as they were required to be snitches. But for the numble singer and dancer, the sailers had the highest esteem. She was "universally respected by the ship's company."

Captain Evans gave her the name Sara. He chose a biblical name, lining the enslaved woman, who was likely an Igbo speaker, to a princess, the beautiful wife of Abraham. Perhaps the captain hoped that she would share other traits with the biblical Sarah, who remained submissive and obedient to her husband during a long journey to Canaan.

`Soon the enslaved men of the Hudibras erupted in insurrection. The goal was to "massacre the ship's company, and take possession of the vessel." The rising was suppressed, bloody punishments dispensed. Afterward Captain Evans and other officers suspected that Sarah and her mother (who was also on board) were somehow involved, even though the women had not joined the men in the actual revolt. When questioned closely, with violence looming, they denied having any knowledge, but "fear, or guilt, was strongly marked on their countenances." Later that night, as male and female captives angrily shout recriminations around the ship in the aftermath of defeat, it became clear that both Sarah and her mother not only know about the plot, they had indeed been involved in it. Sarah had likely used her privileged position as a favorite, and her great freedom of movement that this entailed, to help with planning and perhaps even to pass tools to the men, allowing them to hack off their shackles and manacles.

Sarah survived the Middle Passage and whatever punishment she may have gotten for her involvement in the insurrection. She was sold at Grenada, with almost three hundred others, in 1787. She was allowed to stay on the vessel longer than most, probably with the special permission of Captain Evans. When she went ashore, she carried African traditions of dance, song, and resistance with her.[6][97] (Rediker 19-20)

The movie "Amistad" was one of the best portrayals depicting the conditions and inhuman treatment suffered by illegally captured Africans in America during the Trans-Atlantic Slave Trade. Their imprisonment and trial brought some of the best legal minds in America together to defend Africans.

"In 1839, Portuguese slave traders abducted a group of West Africans from the region now known as Sierra Leone. They were then transported to Havana in Cuba aboard a slave ship called the Tecora. Once in Havana, fifty three of the Africans were sold to two Spanish planters, Pedro Montes and Jose Ruiz. The men planned to take the Africans to Puerto Principe in Cuba aboard a schooner, called the Amistad (ironically meaning friendship). But the Africans aboard the schooner rebelled and took control of the ship. Led by Sengbe Pieh (Cinque), they ordered Montes and Ruiz to sail them to Africa, but instead they sailed along the coast of the US. The Amistad was seized off the coast of Long Island in New York by the USS Washington, a naval ship. The Spanish crews were freed and the Africans were imprisoned in New Haven on charges of murder. Black and white Christian abolitionists, headed mostly by wealthy New York merchant Lewis Tappan, formed the Amistad Committee, which rallied to raise funds for the legal defence of the Africans. Although the murder charges were dismissed in the lower courts, in 1841 the case went to the United States Supreme Court, where it was defended by former President John Quincy Adams, and the court ruled that the Africans aboard the Amistad had been illegally held as slaves. Later that year the Amistad Committee returned 35 Amistad survivors to Africa. The others had died at sea or in prison while awaiting trial."[98] (Library of Congress)

The last Slave ship believed to have brought illegally captured Slaves to America was the Wanderer. This particular Slave ship is of interest to me, because a Slave by the name of Flora Slaver was brought from Africa to Georgia in the mid 1800s. Flora was my great great great great maternal grandmother. I have another ship to search the records for leads to my family's ancestry. The shipment of approximately 400 Slaves were dropped off in Georgia at Jekyll Island in 1858. It was illegal to bring any Slaves to America by that date. The greedy Slave captain ignored the law. It is ironic that this particular Slave ship was captured during the Civil war and was used in the fight to end Slavery.

The Maritime museum in Liverpool England has an archive and library. I was allowed to take pictures of Slave trade records containing information about the Slave ship records from the Slave trade. The following pictures contain information about Slave ship cargo including the number of Slaves on board, and the numbers that survived and died during the voyages. Other records mention Slaves in wills and as property.

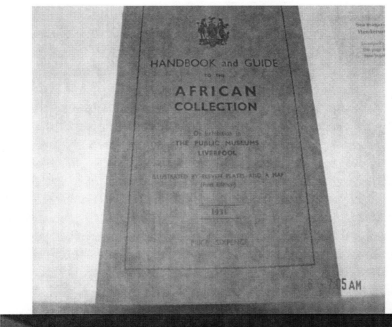

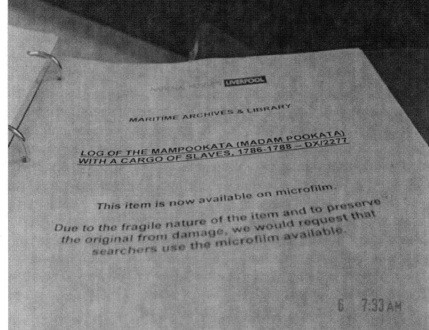

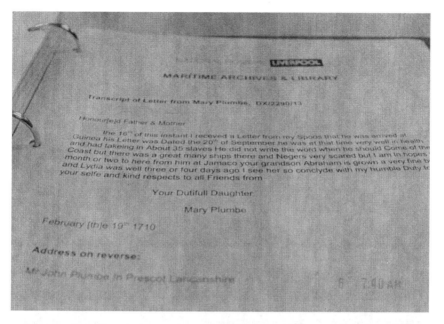

LIVERPOOL

MARITIME ARCHIVES & LIBRARY

Transcript of Letter from Mary Plumbe, DX/2290/1

Honoured Father & Mother

the 16th of this instant I receved a Letter from my Spoos that he was arrived at Guinea his Letter was Dated the 20th of September he was at that time very well in health and had takeing in About 35 slaves He did not write the word when he should Come of the Coast but there was a great many ships there and Negers very scared but I am in hopes month or two to here from him at Jamaco your grandson Abraham is grown a very fine boy and Lydia was well three or four days ago I see her so conclyde with my humble Duty to your selfe and kind respects to all Friends from

Your Dutifull Daughter

Mary Plumbe

February [th]e 19th 1710

Address on reverse:

Mr John Plumbe in Prescot Lancunshire

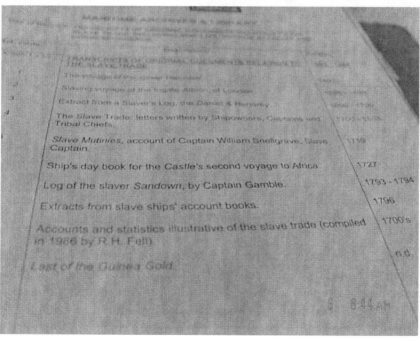

MARITIME ARCHIVES & LIBRARY

TRANSCRIPTS OF ORIGINAL DOCUMENTS RELATING TO THE SLAVE TRADE.

The voyage of the slaver Hannibal.

Slaving voyage of the frigate Albion of London.

Extract from a Slaver's Log, the Daniel & Henry.

The Slave Trade: letters written by Shipowners, Captains and Tribal Chiefs.

Slave Mutinies, account of Captain William Snelgrave, Slave Captain.

Ship's day book for the Castle's second voyage to Africa

Log of the slaver Sandown, by Captain Gamble.

Extracts from slave ships' account books.

Accounts and statistics illustrative of the slave trade (compiled in 1986 by R H. Fell)

Last of the Guinea Gold.

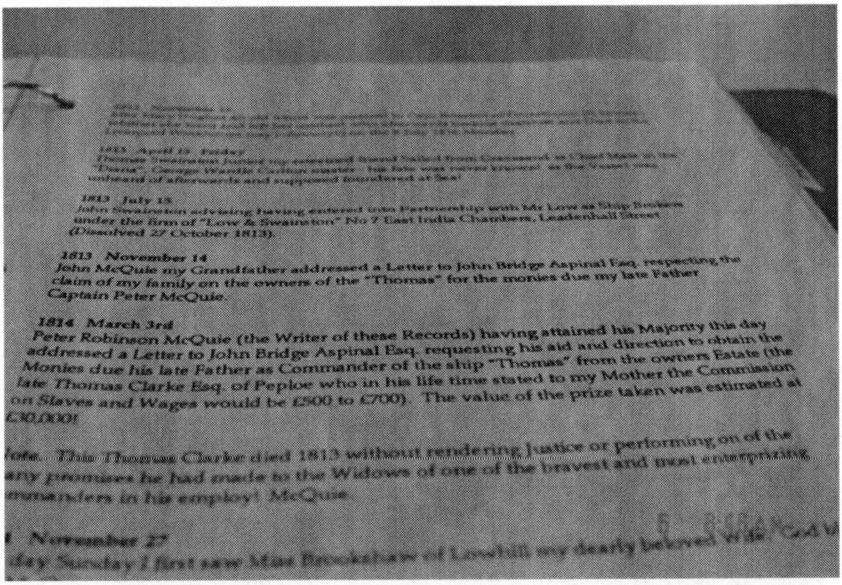

1813 September 1x
[illegible faded text]

1813   April 13   Friday
Thomas Swainston Joined my command board failed from Gravesend as Chief Mate in the
"Davis", George Wardle Carlton master – his fate was never known as first Vessel was
unheard of afterwards and supposed foundered at Sea!

1813   July 18
John Swainston advising having entered into Partnership with Mr Low as Ship Brokers
under the firm of "Low & Swainston" No 7 East India Chambers, Leadenhall Street
(Dissolved 27 October 1813).

1813   November 14
John McQuie my Grandfather addressed a Letter to John Bridge Aspinal Esq. respecting the
claim of my family on the owners of the "Thomas" for the monies due my late Father
Captain Peter McQuie.

1814   March 3rd
Peter Robinson McQuie (the Writer of these Records) having attained his Majority this day
addressed a Letter to John Bridge Aspinal Esq. requesting his aid and direction to obtain the
Monies due his late Father as Commander of the ship "Thomas" from the owners Estate (the
late Thomas Clarke Esq. of Peploe who in his life time stated to my Mother the Commission
on Slaves and Wages would be £500 to £700). The value of the prize taken was estimated at
£30,000!

Note. This Thomas Clarke died 1813 without rendering Justice or performing, on of the
any promises he had made to the Widows of one of the bravest and most enterprising
commanders in his employ! McQuie.

November 27
[illegible] Sunday I first saw Miss Brookshaw of Lowhill my dearly beloved Wife [illegible]

REEL 10   D/EARLE/1/1-7 (continued)

got 350 slaves rather than risk your own lives by such long detention, and
what goods remain lay out for Teeth of any size if possible and then proceed
to Barbados and apply to Mr Sam Carter merchant there who will advise
you the state of prices for slaves at the other islands from which you will
Judge whether to proceed further or stop there. If you go to Antigua apply
to Messrs George and Ralph Walker and Mr Andrew Lesley. If to St Kitts
Messrs Guichard and Scarret, Messrs Payne and Leigh any of which will
make the most in Sales give the Earliest desatch and Best remittances where
you set down we recommend your agreeing for and fixing the Exchange on
Bills and time the shall be remitted for the balance and if Possible all of the
ships, this not being done give room for advancing the Exchange when such
remittances are to be made which lessens our interest greatly.

If none of our islands offer to Incourage you calling Proceed directly to
Barbados to St Eustatia and if you can obtain £17 sterling per head [illegible]
with full remittance in good bills at Thirty, Forty or Sixty [illegible]
any offered [illegible]

DX/1543	Receipt for return of allowance paid to staff officer James Wilson, Apothecary to the forces at the Garrison of Zenegal for a black servant from 1 July- 30 Sept 1811
DX/1544	Letter from James Calley Manager of a Plantation in Berbice, Guiana to his Proprietor Hugh McCalmont in Belfast. He reports on the estate, cotton bales, negro slaves, ginning machinery, other neighbouring estates & asks for further instructions, 18 August 1826
DX/1550 (R)	Printed volume. Substance of the Report of the Sierra Leone Company includes map of the area, plantations & general comments on the slave trade. 1794
DX/1551	Notice of a Charleston Auction of 25 Sea Island Cotton & Rio Negro Slaves, 1852. Agreement for sale of a female slave, N Orleans 1853 (with transcript) & receipt for all items bought antique shop in New Orleans. 1964

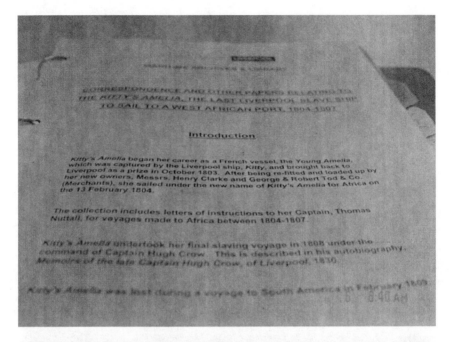

CORRESPONDENCE AND OTHER PAPERS RELATING TO THE KITTY'S AMELIA, THE LAST LIVERPOOL SLAVE SHIP TO SAIL TO A WEST AFRICAN PORT, 1804-1807

Introduction

Kitty's Amelia began her career as a French vessel, the *Young Amelia*, which was captured by the Liverpool ship, *Kitty*, and brought back to Liverpool as a prize in October 1803. After being re-fitted and loaded up by her new owners, Messrs. Henry Clarke and George & Robert Tod & Co. (Merchants), she sailed under the new name of *Kitty's Amelia* for Africa on the 13 February 1804.

The collection includes letters of instructions to her Captain, Thomas Nuttall, for voyages made to Africa between 1804-1807.

Kitty's Amelia undertook her final slaving voyage in 1808 under the command of Captain Hugh Crow. This is described in his autobiography, *Memoirs of the late Captain Hugh Crow, of Liverpool, 1830*.

Kitty's Amelia was lost during a voyage to South America in February 1809.

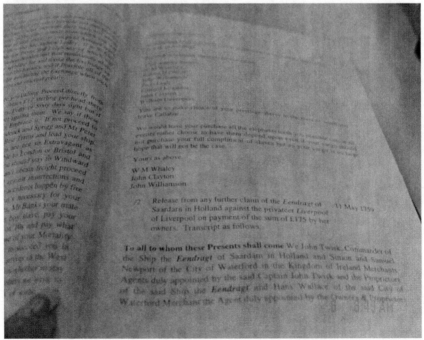

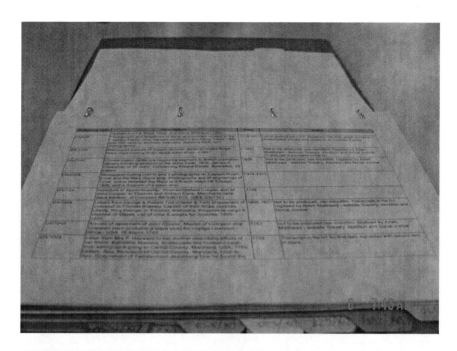

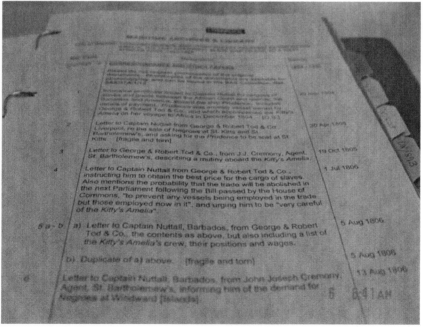

"... to the Eternal disgrace of the Navy who ... because those
of this kind in the Mercht service ... them in the road of being
Confined, where incaraged to it by the Officers of the Schooner
& there Agent, a well-known Infamous Caracter in St. Kitts,
one Doctor Armstrong, to bring this Accusation against the
Capt. for the main purpose on their side of confounding & per-
plexing him & thereby extrol more readily the penalty for A
pretended Overplus of Slaves said to be brought by his Orders
in the brig *Prudence*. This his an Affair of more Serious Conse-
quance to the Underwriters than perhaps they are Aware of,
as had Nuttall not Acted as he did they would most Certainly
have had to be Answerable to you for the Ship & Cargo, &
instances are not wanting to shew where they have paid Severely
for Similliar Acts of Piracy. I therefore hope & trust that in
this Case you will use your endeavours with that Very respectable
Body, and at last Obtain for Nuttal an indemnity of the expenc
he as been at as a reward for that Merit wich Appeer'd so Hono
able to him at the Tril in Saving the Propperty in so Crit
a Moment as well as the Lives of the Innocent whe of Neccess
must have been lost in attempting to withstand so Darin

...
Dear Sir, yours sincerely,

The next letter to the Captain was dated 5th August.

DEAR NUTTALL, Annexed is a Dupt. of what we wrote you
the 1st ult., to which we have nothing particular to add. The
Bill has now passed to prevent any more vessels from going to
Africa, but those already in the Trade, and there can be no
change of property whatever in them after the 1st inst. It is
very fully expected that it will be totally abolished next Session.
We have therefore great expectations from your present voyage,
and herewith enclose a P/C for your Govt. If you sell at Barba-
does, and there is anything you conceive will pay, (you) may
take a part in Produce, but would prefer Bills if at moderat
dates. As we have so many Guarantees for that Island, coul
you not dispose of your Cargo to them in lots free of Commissio
taking their Bills on Barrow & Co. for the Amount. Sho
you go to Trinidad we wish you to take all in Bills unless Proc
is very low and likely to leave a handsome profit. If a
... Govt. Bills, we wis

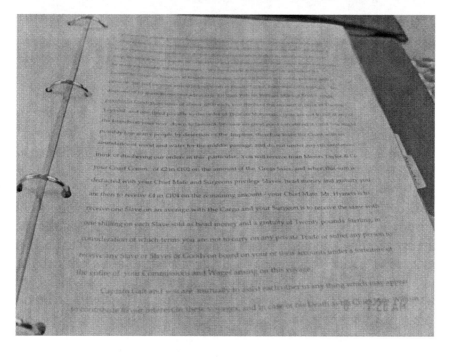

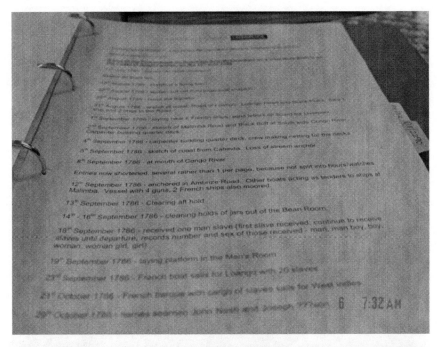

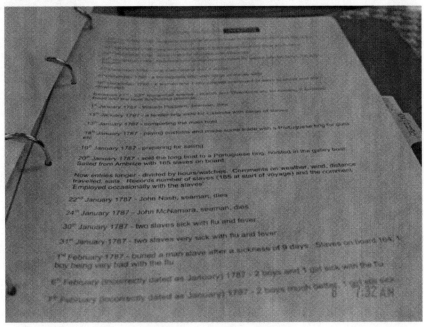

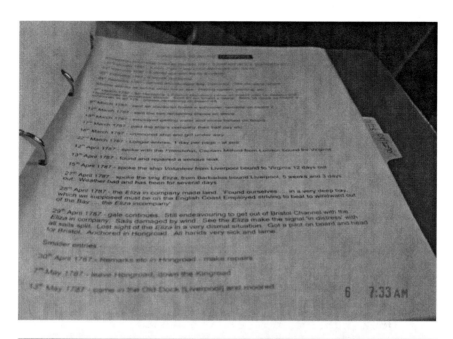

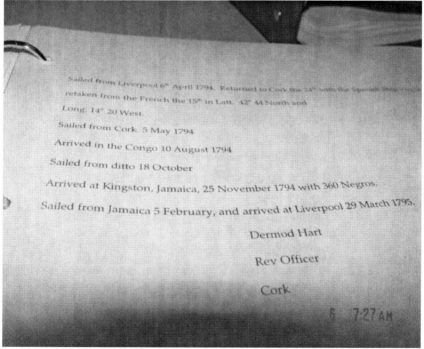

Sailed from Liverpool 6th April 1794. Returned to Cork the 24th with the Spanish Ship being retaken from the French the 15th in Latt. 42° 44 North and Long. 14° 20 West.

Sailed from Cork 5 May 1794

Arrived in the Congo 10 August 1794

Sailed from ditto 18 October

Arrived at Kingston, Jamaica, 25 November 1794 with 360 Negros.

Sailed from Jamaica 5 February, and arrived at Liverpool 29 March 1795.

Dermod Hart

Rev Officer

Cork

The following chart is a timeline calendar highlighting important dates and events significant to European and American involvement and abolishment of the Slave trade.

CHRONOLOGY OF THE SLAVE TRADE

1441	Portuguese sailors take the first shipload of Africans to Europe as slaves.
1444	First large group of enslaved Africans brought to Europe.
1482	Elmina Castle (one of the most known slave trading forts in West Africa) built by the Portuguese; first European fort built on the Gold Coast.
1498	Columbus takes black slaves to Hispaniola.
1502	First record of African slave in the New World.
1510	King Ferdinand authorizes the shipment of a group of Africans to Santo Domingo, thus beginning systematic importation of slaves into the New World.
1517	First Importation of Africans into Jamaica.
1518	First black cargo direct from Africa arrives in the West Indies.
1538	First Negro slaves brought to Brazil.
1562	Sir John Hawkins sets out on his first slaving voyage.
1607	The Dutch West India Company is established and dominates early slave trade to the Americas.
1619	The first black slaves are shipped to the English Colony of Jamestown, Virginia.
1621	The Dutch West India Company granted monopoly over the Dutch African slave trade.

1637	Elmina Castle is captured by the Dutch who keeps it for the next two centuries.
1663	King Charles II sets up the Company of Royal Adventures to trade with Africa.
1672	King Charles II forms the Royal African Company to control the English slave trade after the Company of Royal Adventures ran into debt problems.
1698	Act passes, which ends the Royal African Company monopoly.
1759	The abolitionist, William Wilberforce, is born.
1760	Thomas Clarkson, the abolitionist, is born.
1770s	Abolitionist Granville Sharpe dedicates his time to collecting evidence against slavery.
1772	The Mansfield Judgement frees English slaves.
1783	An abolition bill is debated on moral grounds in the House of Commons but fails to get majority support.
1787	The Society for the Abolition of the Slave Trade is formed in London.
1788	William Pitt orders investigation of the slave trade. First debates on the British slave trade in parliament.
1789	William Wilberforce delivers his first abolition speech in parliament.
1791	Wilberforce makes motion in the House of Commons to introduce an abolition bill but is unsuccessful.
1791-92	Second Maroon War in Jamaica.

1791-1804	Haitian revolt against slavery and the trade in humans, which effectively inspires and increases the abolition trade.
1792	House of Commons votes in favour of the abolition but is rejected by the House of Lords. Denmark becomes the first country to pass a law abolishing the slave trade.
1793-1802	French revolutionary War between Britain and France effectively delays the abolition campaign.
1794	France passes initial laws abolishing slave trade. Legislation is passed by US Congress to prevent US vessels being used in the slave trade.
1796	House of Commons decides to end the British slave trade but the passing of an abolition bill is delayed.
1804	Haiti achieves its independence and becomes the first free nation in the Caribbean.
1806	Britain bans the sale of slaves to foreign colonies.
1807	Abolition Bill passes in the British House of Lords in March and becomes a law in May. US ban the slave trade, to take effect the following year. Britain declares Sierra Leone a Crown Colony.
1814	Holland passes law abolishing slave trade.
1816	Easter Rebellion in Barbados.

1818	France outlaws the slave trade.
1820	Spain abolishes the slave trade.
1831-32	Christmas rebellions in St. James, Jamaica, led by Samuel Sharpe gives monumentum to the anti-slavery movement.
1834	Britain abolishes slavery in the British Empire.

[99] (National Library of Jamaica)

Interviews

Marlene and her Pastor Rev. Dr. Charles G. Adams

Dr. Charles G. Adams is the Sr. Pastor of Hartford Memorial Baptist Church. He is also a professor at Harvard

University. Dr. Adam's insight as a respected world renowned theologian was sought to answer questions about Christians and Christianities' responsibility for the Slave trade. The interview with Dr. Adams was quite extensive, so excerpts from the interview are noted in this Dissertation.

Dr. Charles G. Adams' Interview

Dr. Adams was asked to share his thoughts about the role Christians and Christianity played in the Slave trade.

"It is so well documented that Slavery took place with the affirmation, and the support of the Christian Church particularly the church in Europe, the British Isles and of course in Spain. There is a clear record in fact it would be very unusual if one could find any church of any denomination that did not participate in the very lucrative traffic in human flesh. Dr. Adams said that would be quite the exception. As in the case of the Quakers, the Quakers did not participate in war or in Slavery. There might have been some others who did not participate because of pacifistic feelings. People like the Moravians who felt that the Bible just did not condone it, and therefore they would not do it. But unless there were people who had the kind of faith that would go against the prevailing society, the prevailing economics, and the prevailing culture, they participated in the Slave trade. It was quite evident that all the Churches and certainly European based churches that we have known in this country every one of them with the exception of the Quakers practiced Slavery.

That's why you had, and of course the churches that came together were beginning to feel like the Quakers, with the exception of the churches in the south. The Methodist in the south and the Methodist in the north and the Baptist in the south and the Baptist in the north are still separated. That is why they separated in 1845 on the very issue of Slavery. Some of the churches were coming around and beginning to feel like the Quakers. They could not be Christians and Slave owners at the same time. There were those in the south who built their whole culture and their whole economy on the fact that they were getting free Slave labor. The millions of Slaves that were brought here to America were not to enjoy freedom, not to enjoy the full recognition of their humanity, and not to enjoy an education. They were brought here to work. They were brought here to form the foundation of the United States economy and very largely the world economy based on the dehumanization of the people and Slavery of these people. You would have to strain to find any majoritarian Christian people who took a courageous stand against Slavery. The bishop of London in 1667 said "you can preach the gospel to the Slaves, but they must remain Slaves. There freedom must be a freedom from sin, and their own lust, and inordinate desires." "But as to Slavery, they are still Slaves." So you found people who were willing even to distort the word of God and to poison the Constitution of the United States with the recognition of the legality of slavery based upon there reduction of the humanity of the Slaves and to say that Slaves were only 3/5ths human. It is the other side that must prove not Christians, but those who would dare think that Christianity did no perpetuate and participate in Slavery, or those who dare think that Christians did no create Slavery. They were willing to back Slavery with guns and armies to protect Slavery. If you were a Slave and escaped, they would use the law, soldiers, and poses to bring you back to the Slave owner and re-enslave you. These are the facts that we must face." [100] (Adams)

Janet Butler and Marlene

Janet Butlers' Interview

Janet Butler repatriated to Accra Ghana to live. She is originally from New York City. Janet moved to Accra with her husband and children two years ago. They lived in Nigeria for five years prior to moving to Accra. Janet always wanted to live in Africa. Her husband was a law student in Ghana. They had different paths that lead them to Africa. Janet's job transferred her to Nigeria. The experience was so positive that she and her husband decided to organize themselves and planned to move to Ghana.

They have a good support network of Lawyers. Every year the African Americans from the United States celebrate Black History month. The cultural festival was a culmination of the month's activities. Africans and African Americans come together.

Janet's opinion on the slave trade was partially based on what happened to her when she moved to Nigeria. Her family includes a great grand mother from Nigeria. When Janet moved to Nigeria, because of the hue of her skin, they considered her a white person. Ghanaians don't relate to the Slave trade, because they don't fill it has anything to do with them. The Africans' disconnect from the Slave trade history was shocking to Janet.

Janet visited Slave sites on Goree Island, and Benin, which has a commemorative archway remaining. She also visited Cape Coast and Elmina castles numerous times. None of those places affected her like Elmina. That was the first Castle she visited. No matter how distant you believe that history is, when you go in the dungeon, the history is in your face. She thought she could hear and feel the people. Janet was fortunate because she knows her father's paternal side is traced to Nigeria. Her great grandmother came from the middle belt of Nigeria. Other than that, she never really thought about her families' beginning. Past that family history, she claims all of Africa. Janet and her husband wanted an environment where their family could be free. It is the greatest gift they could give to their children.

If someone is thinking about moving to Africa, they should visit for an extended amount of time, and not as a tourist. Do your homework as Janet suggest. Make sure you have a secure source of income, property in the States to live on, or try to get a one year visa to do business. Don't be arrogant, as many African American have been. If you think you are bringing something special, you may be disappointed. Don't think the people of Africa are uneducated. Janet recommends that people look around to see where they might fit in. Partner with Ghanaians whenever possible to gain insight. Some African Americans believe that Ghana offers dual citizenship; it is not true Janet says. Indefinite stays may be granted if you are married to a Ghanaian for two years. The marriage allows you to live there and own land even if you do not stay with the person you married. You can do everything but vote. Then you won't have to get a visa every year. Janet also shared that if you are an African American from the Diaspora, the right of abode may be granted if you reside in Ghana for seven years. You need character references and must prove that you are an asset to Ghana, and can survive monetarily.

Surveys

The Trans-Atlantic Slave trade and Christianity are subjects that start great debates and discussions. The following survey was given to volunteers of different genders, races, and socio economic classes. A number of individuals volunteered to fill out the survey titled "Slavery and Christianity, the Untold Story. A copy of the survey is followed by a completed one from a volunteer who did not mind identifying herself. A chart was prepared to categorize totals for some of the answers to the survey questions.

"SLAVERY AND CHRISTIANITY THE UNTOLD STORY" SURVEY

Date:_____/_____/_____

Thank you in advance for participating in this survey. Your participation may assist others in initiating a search for their family
lineage and encourage closer relationships with existing family members.

(Personal Identification Optional)

Name
optional:_____

Occupation_____

Title_____

What is your opinion of the African Trans-Atlantic Slave Trade?

_____
_____
_____
_____
_____
_____

Have you heard of the slave castles and forts of Africa? Yes____NO____

What do you know about the slave castles and forts of Africa?_____

_____

_____

_____

Have you visited a slave castle or forts in Africa?
Yes_____No?_____
How many have you
visited?_____

Which slave castles or forts have you
visited?_____

How many times have you visited the slave castles or forts?_____

What were your experiences during your visit(s)?_____

_____

_____

_____

_____

_____

_____

Did you go through the door of no return?
Yes_____No_____
How did you feel and what did you experience?_____

_____

_____

_____

_____

_____

Did the Slave castle or fort have a church on the premises? Yes___No__
What denomination was it?
Christian_____Museum_____other_____
_____
Was the church located in the same building as the slave dungeons or in a separate building?
_____
How did you feel visiting a church on the grounds of a slave castle or
fort?_____

_____
_____
_____
_____
_____

How many generations has your family been traced to on your mothers side of the
family?_____
On your fathers side of the
family?_____
Do you know where your family originated?
Yes_____No_____
What is the country of your family's'
origin?_____
If you have traced your family to Africa, what country and
tribe?_____

_____
_____
_____

Have you or your family traced your family's lineage?
Yes____NO___
Do you care to know where your family originated?
Yes___NO___
_____
Does your family hold family reunions?
Yes_____No_____
How often are family reunions held for your
family?_____ Mother's
family_____
Father's
family_____
Are you a Christian? Yes_____No_____If not
what religion do you practice or believe
in?_____
Do you believe Christians or Christianity was
partially responsible or played a role in the
enslavement of the African people? Yes____No____
Why or why
not?_____
_____
_____
_____
_____
_____
Do you believe the enslaved African's descendants are
entitled to reparations?
Yes_____No?_____
What type of reparations would you suggest?
Do you believe they are entitled to an apology?
Yes_____No_____ Who should make the

apology?_____

Do you have any other thoughts that you would like to share regarding the Trans-Atlantic Slave Trade? ____

_____
_____
_____
_____
_____
_____
_____
_____
_____

"SLAVERY AND CHRISTIANITY THE UNTOLD STORY" SURVEY

Date:____/____/_____

Thank you in advance for participating in this survey. Your participation may assist others in initiating a search for their family history, or encourage closer relationships with existing family members.

(Name and Personal Identification Optional)

Name optional: Dawn L. Holt_____

Occupation   Healthcare_____

Title: Patient Coordinator_____

What is your opinion of the African Trans-Atlantic Slave Trade?
It was a dreadful time in history for not just Africans, but all involved.

_____
_____
_____
_____
_____

Have you heard of the slave castles and forts of Africa? Yes__ NO___ What do you know about the

**slave castles and forts of
Africa?**_____

_____

_____

_____

**Have you visited a slave castle or forts in Africa?
Yes_____No_____**

**How many have you
visited?**_____

**Which slave castles or forts have you
visited?**_____

**How many times have you visited the slave castles or
slave forts?**_____

What were your experience during your visit(s)?____

_____

_____

_____

_____

**Did you go through the door of no return?
Yes_____No_____**

How did you feel and what did you experience?_____

_____

_____

_____

_____

**Did the Slave castle or fort have a church on the
premises?Yes____No__**

What denomination was it?
Christian_____Muselum_____other_____
Was the church located in the same building as the
slave dungeons or in a separate building?
_____
How did you feel visiting a church on the grounds of a
slave castle or
fort?_____
_____
_____
_____
_____
_____

How many generations has your family been traced to
on your mothers side of the family?
_____**5 or 6**_____
On your fathers side of the
family?_____**5**_____
Do you know where your family originated?
Yes_____**No**_____
What is the country of your family's'
origin?_____
If you have traced your family to Africa, what
country and
tribe?_____
_____
_____
_____

Have you or your family traced your family's lineage?
Yes____**NO**___

Do you care to know where your family originated?
Yes___NO___
_____

Does your family hold family reunions?
Yes_____No_____
How often are family reunions held for your family?
_____Annually or every other year_____
Mother's family _____annually_____
Father's family___Every other year____
_____

**Are you a Christian? Yes_____No_____If not
what religion do you practice or believe
in?_____
Do you believe Christians or Christianity was
partially responsible or played a role in the
enslavement of the African people? Yes___No___
Why or why not? My answer changed recently when I
was exposed to reading materials which discussed the
role of religion in slavery. After significant research, I
feel that Christianity was once considered a "white
man's religion" and that slaves were forced to adopt it
once they were purchased.**
_____
_____
_____
_____
_____
_____

**Do you believe the enslaved African's descendants are
entitled to reparations?**
Yes_____No?_____

What type of reparations would you suggest? While I believe they are entitled to reparations, I do not feel that there is any form of reparation that can make up for the actions of those involved.

Do you believe they are entitled to an apology?

Yes _____ **No** _____ **Who should make the apology?** Unfortunately, the people who truly owe the apology are long gone. Some Whites may feel obligated to apologize for "their people" but it is not their responsibility to do so they can apologize by discontinuing the mindset which caused the slavery in the first place

Do you have any other thoughts that you would like to share regarding the Trans-Atlantic Slave Trade? I feel that more education should be offered regarding this and other "Black History" – not just to Blacks out to all students. I believe that this would decrease racism in younger generations because they could begin to understand the significance of the African-American struggle.

Survey Totals

Heard of Slave Castles and Forts of Africa	Visited Slave Castles and Forts in Africa	Average # of Generations traced Matriarchally	Average # of Generations traced Patriarchally	Traced your family to Africa
Female	Female	Female	Female	Female
28	9	4	3	6
Male	Male	Male	Male	Male
7	6	2	3	5

Does your family have family reunions	How often are family reunions held for your family Every year? Every two years?	Do you believe the enslaved African's descendants are entitled to reparations	Do you believe Christians or Christianity was partially responsible or played a role in the enslavement of the African people	Do you care about your Genealogy?
Female	Female	Female	Female	Female
Yes 35	Every Year? 28	Yes 40	Yes 41	Yes 38
No 6	Every other year? 13	No 1	No 0	No 3
Total 41	Total 41	Total 41	Total 41	Total 41

Male		Male		Male		Male		Male	
Yes	17	Every Year?	14	Yes	20	Yes	21	Yes	14
No	4	Every other year?	9	No	1	No	0	No	7
Total	21	Total	23	Total	21	Total	21	Total	21

Endnotes:

(90) Joseph Project Souvenir Book - Ghana Ministry of Tourism 2007- (Page 3)

(91) The Mariners' Museum - 2002

(92) Hanson 14

(93) The Mariners' Museum – 2002

(94) The Mariners' Museum - 2002

(95) The Slave Ship A Human History Marcus Rediker - 2007 The Penquin Group - NY NY (Page 17-18)

(96) The Slave Ship A Human History Marcus Rediker - 2007 The Penquin Group - NY NY (Page 16)

(97) The Slave Ship A Human History Marcus Rediker - 2007 The Penquin Group - NY NY (Page 19-20)

(98) Library of Congress

(99) Chronology of the Slave Trade National Library of Jamaica – 2007

(100) Interview – Dr. Charles G. Adams – 2008

CHAPTER VI

Breaking the Chains of Slavery and Healing the Nations

Repentance, apologies, and forgiveness are necessary to heal the historical open wounds and evils of the Trans-Atlantic Slave trade. The Slave trade left the earmarks of hatred, racism, and discrimination on the enslaved African descendants throughout the world.

This dissertation is intended to be part of the solution to breaking the chains of silence connected to the pre-middle passage history of the enslavement of Africans. Acknowledgement of the truth about the horrible Trans-Atlantic Slave trade past by descendants, governments, and monarchies responsible for the crimes against humanity followed by apologies, reconciliation, and communication between all parties are recipes for peace and forgiveness. Young people should not take for granted the right to get an education and strive to do and be the best in life. It means little to some and more to others to take responsibility for one's actions. The descendants of the Slave traders and owners must decide for themselves if taking responsibility for what their ancestors did to the African people means anything.

Who should the enslaved African descendants claim as their country men and women? What is their country? Where is their hope? Do not focus solely on copying others, be yourself. What God does for the people you admire, He can also do for you. The people who suffered and died for what Slavery meant should provide added motivation for all men and women of color to do their best. Take the best of the African heritage and of the European, and the Americas, and rise above any persons opinion, any persons ways, and any person's none acceptance of you. God and the individual's opinions are the only ones that count. Oppressors may kill the body, but they can not kill what does not belong to them, your soul. One must learn to avert the person or people that are keeping them down or bound.

Ghana's' Panafest cultural event is one endeavor to inform,

reconcile, heal, re-connect, and bring enslaved African descendants through out the Diaspora home to Africa every two years. The truth is an important component to healing the open wounds of Slavery and moving forward. This dissertation is intended to inspire dreams, awaken a consciousness, and provide redirection for the decisions people make in their lifetime. We all "stand on the shoulders of our ancestors".

"Now the Lord is that Spirit: and where the spirit of the Lord is, there is liberty."[101] (2 Corinthians 3:17)

> "Panafest can be described as a logical extension of the PAN-AFRICANIST movement whose inspiration gave birth to Ghana in 1957 and equally closed the door to APARTHEID in South Africa. The idea of the celebration of the PANAFEST was first mooted by the late Dr. (Mrs.) Efua Sunderland, a dramatist and Pan-Africanist in 1980. It was in a written form entitled "PROPOSAL FOR A HISTORICAL IN CAPE COAST". In 1991, the idea gained ground and PANAFEST was launched in the same year at Cape Coast." [102] (Ghana Ministry of Tourism 68-69)

What an honor it is to be alive at such a time in history to bear witness to the first African American presidential nominee, and to witness people of all races, cultures and socioeconomic classes come together for "change." Change could be the acronym for Christ Has Answered, Now God's Eternal. Will African descendants ever really be treated as equals? Will that ever really happen? Yes when Jesus returns. Should the descendants forget what happened to the African ancestors? Is there too much pain and anger to release the conditions of the past? It is most certainly easy to say yes if you are not a victim of continued racism and discrimination. Reconciliation is one of the answers for those who have been and are victims in spite of society.

The Golden Jubilee of Ghana's Independence, Panafest, and the 200th anniversary of the Abolishment of Slavery were recognized in 2007 during the Joseph Project activities in Ghana in 2007.

The following is the welcome address by the President of Ghana. His words of wisdom surmises the steps needed to heal some of the hurts and injustice continuously stinging the enslaved African descendants throughout the Diaspora and in Africa from the Trans-Atlantic Slave trade.

"THE. John Agyekum Kufuor-President of Ghana" "I welcome you to this year's activities aimed at reuniting the African Family. This year is special as it coincides with very important events for us. First of all, the 200th Anniversary Of The Abolition Of The North Atlantic Slave Trade which remains the greatest example in history of man's inhumanity to man.

The other activity of special importance to us is our Golden Jubilee. 50 years ago, we led the way and inspired others to fight for the emancipation of Africans world wide. Today, we are at the forefront of efforts to change the perception about our brothers and sisters in the Diaspora and to reconnect with them I urge you all to use this period to bond with each other because with our combined efforts, we will be better placed to develop the Motherland."[103] (Ghana Ministry of Tourism 10)

Let us not forget that Apartied ended in South Africa less than twenty years ago. Steven Biko sacrificed his life for the freedom of South Africans. Biko said,

"I think it is possible to adapt to a given hard situation precisely because you have got to live it, and you have got to live with it every day. But adapting does not mean that you forget; you go to the mill every day, it is always unacceptable to you, it has always been unacceptable to you, and it remains so for life, but you adapt in the sense that you cannot live in a state of conflict with yourself. Emancipation, on the other hand, is only possible when those who would be free accept the inevitability of their liberation.

This, ultimately is the message of Bantu Steve Biko" [104] (Biko 10)

Old Apartied Court Room in South Africa

Robbin Island

The bed Nelson Mandela slept on while imprisoned on Robbin Island for 27 years

Bill and Marlene on the Dock of a previous Slave Trade Port in
Amsterdam

Based on the cold weather we were experiencing in
Amsterdam in March 2008, it was hard for Bill to imagine what
the Slaves suffered.   As he stood on the docks where Slave ships
once docked in Amsterdam, he couldn't imagine not having any
shoes, or being wrapped in very little clothing. Even worse, maybe
the Slaves were wet from the climate, having traveled from the
coast of Ghana. It was a unique experience for him to be able to
picture the Africans traveling from Africa on Slave ships to
Amsterdam and other countries.

Museum of History in Barcelona Spain

Apologies

There have been apologies from National Leaders and Presidents of Countries directly involved in enslaving the African people. Surprisingly, no formal apology has come from the President of the United States directly to the enslaved Africans and their descendents who helped build the infrastructures and wealth of America. At one time, reparations were granted to freed Slaves in America. Laws were passed to rescind the decision.

"From the historical perspective, it seems clear that the slave issue was the driving force behind the struggle for Ghana's independence. The idea to establish self governance for Africans has been the dream of many descendants of African slaves in America and the West Indies."

Among them were Garvey Marcus Moziah, W. E. B. Du Bois and George Padmore. Their inspiration and encouragement certainly paved the way for Dr. Kwame Nkrumah and others in Africa to take up the challenge to liberate not only Ghana but also the entire continent of Africa."[105] (Ghana Ministry of Tourism)

Marlene at the grave site of W.E.B Dubois in Accra Ghana

"It is crucial to note that the celebrations to mark the 50th anniversary of Ghana's independence will not be complete without the government issuing an apology for the historic role the ancestors played in the Trans-Atlantic Slave Trade.

Although the British government and the Queen have refused to apologise for the role of their ancestors in the Trans-Atlantic Slave trade, the Archbishop of Canterbury, Dr. Rowan Williams, issued an apology only on behalf of his church but not for the government.

An apology from the Ghana government on the other hand to our kith and kin in the Diaspora will not only be the greatest honour for their recognised role in the struggle for Ghana's independence but will certainly start the process of finally closing and healing the rifts and divisions that persist between Africans and descendants of Africa in the North and South Americas, West Indies, Cuba, Haiti and elsewhere.

An apology will serve as an acknowledgement of the gravity and scale of the crime committed not only against our fellow Africans but also against humanity as a whole. It will certainly pave the way for more equal engagements in all fields between Africans and African descendants in the Diaspora."[106] (Ministry of Tourism)

It was considered immoral to end Slavery by Slave owners in the southern United States. There was a fear that the Slaves might become the masters and they the Slaves. How ironic. The end of slavery could be considered immoral yet Slavery during the Slave trade was justified in the minds of the enslavers! More than an apology is necessary to make up for the suffering. How does one know they are enslaved unless they understand what Slavery entails?

"Late 18th Century Anti Slavery Medallion"

Let God's People Go

"Am I not a woman and a sister?

If the Queen of England won't apologize for England's participation in the Slave trade, maybe she would be willing to admit that the treatment the Africans were subjected to during the Slave trade in her country was brutal and inhumane. Does she not realize what racial healing and forgiveness that might take place throughout the world with just a few words of wisdom in the form of an apology from her?

"January 2, 2003, Queen Elizabeth II of the United Kingdom refused to make a public apology for the long history of Slavery under the British Empire on the basis that it was legal at the time. Writing via assistant private secretary Kay Brock, she said "Under the statute of the International criminal Court, acts of enslavement committed today . . . constitute a crime against humanity. But the historic Slave trade was not a crime against humanity or contrary to international law at the time when the UK government condoned it." Copies of Coke's writings arrived in North America on the Mayflower in 1620, and both John Adams and Patrick Henry cited Coke's treatises to support their revolutionary positions against the Mother Country in the 1770s. Under Lord Coke's leadership, in 1628 the House of Commons forced Charles I of England to accept Coke's Petition of Rights by withholding the revenues the king wanted until he capitulated. The quote is believed to have led to the "castle exception" of self-defense: "A man's house is his castle for where shall a man be safe if it be not in his own house?"[107] (Bowan)

"Liverpool employed more than half of the ships involved in slavery and by the mid 18th century imported annually from Africa more than half of the slaves purchased by all ships in Britain. Its net proceeds from the African trade in 1783-93 were said to be £12,294,116. The profit was accrued on the basis of 878 voyages and the sale of 303,737 slaves. A large part of this profit was returned to a small number of prominent Liverpool men who held both political and economic power. Thomas Johnson was a slave trader who was part owner of slaving ships such as Liverpool Merchant and Blessing. Despite his shameful earnings from the enslavement of Africans, he was described as "the founder of the modern town of Liverpool", served as Mayor of Liverpool in 1695, and an MP from 1701 to 1723, and was even knighted in 1708. Two streets, Sir Thomas Street and Johnson Street, were named after him." [108] (Anti Slavery)

Marlene at the International Slave Museum in Liverpool England

Liverpool Docks where Slaves arrived from West Africa
during the Slave Trade

Prime Minister Tony Blair offered an apology for Britain.
The Royal family had the power to abolish Slavery, but the wealth
they accumulated overshadowed and helped the queen turn a

blinds eye to the atrocities, abuses, rapes, starvations, and mutilations of the African people during the Slave trade.

"THE British Prime Minister, Tony Blair, has apologise for the role his country played in the slave trade.

Tony Blair's apology had come at a time pressure groups were campaigning for a full apology for slavery during the 200th anniversary of British abolition of slave trade.

Tony Blair said there was a legacy from this period of history in Africa and that there was a legacy in relation to Black people living here in Britain."

He said despite the fact that there was no "formal" slave trade in the system today, there were several forms of it, and appealed to the international community to help bring all forms of inhuman activities like discrimination against others to an end." [109] (Achiaw and Twum)

An apology and public acknowledgement of the truth about Africans forcefully brought to America from the Government of the United States of America would heal a lot of broken hearts and open wounds from the Slave trade. Can any amount of money, apologies, or reparations make up for the heinous injustice against the African nations, its people, and the descendants? An acknowledgement and apology would assist this country with removing the mental and physical shackles of racism, injustice, and inequality that afflicts people of color currently.

Reparations

Reparations for the descendants of enslaved Africans have been debated since the abolishment of Slavery.

"The arguments surrounding reparations are based on the formal discussion about reparations and actual land reparations received by African-Americans which were later taken away. In 1865, after the Confederate States of America were defeated in the American Civil War, General William Tecumseh Sherman issued Special Field Orders, No. 15 to solve problems caused by the masses of refugees, a temporary plan granting each freed family forty acres of tillable land in the sea islands and around Charleston, South Carolina for the exclusive use of black people who had been enslaved. The army also had a number of unneeded mules which were given to settlers. Around 40,000 freed slaves were settled on 400,000 acres (1,600 km²) in Georgia and South Carolina. However, President <u>Andrew Johnson</u> reversed the order after <u>Lincoln</u> was assassinated and the land was returned to its previous owners. In <u>1867</u>, <u>Thaddeus Stevens</u> sponsored a bill for the redistribution of land to African Americans, but it was not passed."[110] (Wikipedia)

As a country, we need to deal with the dirty secrets of Slavery. An apology from the President would go a long way with assisting the descendants throughout the African Diaspora and the continent of Africa with reconciliation and possible reparations for the disenfranchisements of people and countries in Africa involved in the Slave trade. Millions of Africans were murdered and died for resisting Slave captures and traders. Tens of Millions died enslaved, were sold multiple times, and beaten for no reason for almost four hundred year. Their suffering is not to be belittled or buried with their bodies.

"Supporters of reparations say that if emancipated slaves had been allowed to possess and retain the profits of their labor, their descendants might now control a much larger share of American social and monetary wealth. Not only did the <u>freedmen</u> and women not receive a share of these profits, but they were stripped of the small amounts of compensation paid to some of them during <u>Reconstruction</u>.

President Ronald Reagan apologized for the Japanese being held against their will in the United States during World War II and provided for reparations to be paid to survivors. Why not the Enslaved African Descendants who are still reaping the ill effects of their ancestors suffering as Slaves? Africans were held in this country and worked for free to build much if its infrastructure.

"Under the <u>Civil Liberties Act of 1988</u>, signed into law by President Ronald Reagan, the U.S. government apologized for <u>Japanese American internment</u> during <u>World War II</u> and provided reparations of $20,000 to each survivor, to compensate for loss of property and liberty during that period. For many years, Native American tribes have received compensation for lands ceded to the United States by them in various treaties. Other countries have also opted to pay reparations for past grievances." (Holocaust Reparations). [111] (Wikipedia)

"Held in Abuja, Nigeria, it laid out Africa's main arguments on the issue. The Abuja Proclamation observed that the damage caused by slavery, colonialism and neo-colonialism "is not a thing of the past, but is painfully manifest in the damaged lives of contemporary Africans from Harlem to Harare, in the damaged economies of the black world from Guinea to Guyana, from Somalia to Suriname." It argued that a moral debt is owed to African peoples and called for "full monetary payment ... through capital transfer and debt cancellation." Subsequently, demands that the slave trade be named a crime against humanity and that the former slave-trading nations apologize for it were woven into the case for reparations.

The campaign received support from some African-American groups in the US, which in a parallel effort were raising the notion of reparations from the US government for the persistence of slavery in that country until the second half of the 19th century. And on the specific issue of an apology, it also gained encouragement from the apology by Pope John Paul II "for the sins of Christian Europe against Africa" during a 1991 visit to Senegal's Gorée Island, one of the main transit centers for the trans-Atlantic slave trade." (Ukabiala 5)

There is a new form of slavery on the horizon. In the United States, the federal and state governments are building fewer schools and more prisons. By no means were the crimes committed justifiable, but the United States has more prisons than any other country in the free world and many of the third world countries. The disproportionate number of minorities, in particularly African American males and females are locked away for longer sentences for the same or lesser crimes of white prisoners. The number of consumer items now produced by prison labor has increased dramatically in recent years. Some of the prisons are contracted out to be privately run. Privately ran prisons may be equivalent to the fox watching the hen house with little oversight.

Endnotes:

(101) (2 Corinthians 3:17)

(102) Joseph Project Souvenir Book - Ghana Ministry of Tourism 2007- (Page 68-69)

(103) Joseph Project Souvenir Book - Ghana Ministry of Tourism

2007- (Page 10)

(104) No Fears Expressed Steve Biko Mutloatse Arts Heritage Trust - 2007 (Page 10)

(105) Breaking the Silence www.antislavery.org All Rights Reserved - Ghana.co.uk - 1999-2001

(106) Joseph Project Souvenir Book - Ghana Ministry of Tourism 2007- (Page 18)

(107) The Lion and the Throne, a biography of Coke February 1552 3 September - 1634- Catherine Drinker Bowen - April 1990

(108) Breaking the Silence www.antislavery.org All Rights Reserved. Ghana.co.uk 1999-2001

(109) Daily Graphic - Nehemiah Owusu Achiaw & Nana Sifa Twum - March 17, 2007

(110) Thirteenth-Amendment to the United States Constitution – Wikipedia March 2007

(111) Holocaust Reparations Wikipedia March 2007

(112) Slave trade 'a crime against humanity' - Jullyette Ukabiala - From Africa Recovery, Vol.15 #3, October 2001 – (page 5)

CHAPTER VII – RECOMMENDATIONS FOR ADDITIONAL RESEARCH

Heart Wrenching Realities

This dissertation only scratched the surface of the pre-middle passage history of the Trans-Atlantic Slave trade. Based on the number of people asked if they were aware of the enslaved African ancestors' history prior to the middle passage, there is a lot of work to be done. The answer was 10 to 1 for limited to no knowledge of pre-middle passage enslaved African history.

The objective to connect Christians and Christianity directly to the Trans-Atlantic Slave trade was sadly verified in this dissertation. From the Christian Church to monarchies of Europe, the butchering, slaughters, discrimination, injustice, and oppression forced upon enslaved Africans during the Slave trade was to a certain extent the work of Christians who used Christianity for ill-gotten gains. Their decisions and greed have unfairly plagued a continent of people and their descendants throughout the Diaspora for almost 400 years.

"As well as for use by colonialists and slave traders, churches were also used to 'christianise' enslaved Africans, who had to be baptised before being loaded onto slave ships like cargo. Churches symbolised oppression and opposition to African religions and practices, and stand as testimony to the violence of enslavement. 'Nossa Senhora do Pópulo is an example of an 18th century church in Benguela."

www.antislavery.org

Benguela is also characterised by its quintalões or 'slave enclosures' that were intended to control enslaved Africans."[113](Anti Slavery)

The dissertation addressed the racial abuse that was and is unfortunately commonly practiced. If you happen to be born to a race of people or of a gender considered inferior in other peoples' opinions, you still can not run for political office, or belong to certain organizations, or vote in some elections. There are different views of what constitutes freedom from the prospective of the oppressed.

"Freedom is so much a part of the human makeup that it is not too far-fetched to say that an un-free human being is in a sense a contradiction in terms. The ideal society is one in which its member enjoy their freedom to be human freely, provided they are not thereby infringe the freedom of others unduly. We are made to have freedom of association, of expression, of movement, the freedom to choose who will rule over us and how. We are made for this. It is ineluctable. It cannot ultimately be eradicated, this yearning for freedom to be human. This is what tyrants and unjust rulers have to contend with. They can not in the end stop their victims from being human." [11](Tutu 45[4])

The countries that absconded land and resources from the African countries forcibly are now selling back to African countries the same resources they forcibly took from them. The pre-middle passage of African history is noticeably absent from being readily accessible to African descendants in America, Europe, and Africa.

The mission to enlighten the world about the Trans-Atlantic Slave trade especially the pre-middle passage history was documented in earlier chapters. Some people have asked what was the middle passage of the Slave trade? Other wanted to know what the triangle trade route was and if it was different from the middle passage. The number of people shocked by the involvement of Christians and Christianity proves that more discussions and information should be made available for the world to know the truth. Being asked by more than one person necessitates the need for further research on the topic of the Slave Trade and the involvement of Christians and Christianity. The request to read this paper was overwhelming. There was a strong interest in learning more about the Slave trade from people in the United States, Africa, and Europe.

There should be an inclusion of the Slave trade history in all American history text books.

Encouragement for the Future

The Atlantic and Indian Oceans join together yet they are separate and equal in strength in South Africa. If only people of the world would accept each other as culturally diverse yet equal as human beings and children created by God.

The Atlantic Ocean and Indian Ocean join together in South Africa

In 1955, Rosa Parks was arrested for refusing to give her seat to a white man on a Montgomery Alabama bus. The Civil Rights movement was officially recognized. Mrs. Park's defiance

also catapulted the mission and ministry of Dr. Martin Luther King Jr. to end racism and discrimination against people of color and women in America.

"I am the product of Africa and her long cherished dream of a rebirth that can now be realized so that all her children may play in the sun."[114] (Mandela)[2]

Portrait of Mandela

Marlene in the Mandela Museum in South Africa

Newer Courtroom at the Constitution Hill Museum in South Africa

Marlene with members of the tribe of her Ancestors, the Asante of Ghana

Worship Service at Miracle Rock Church in Ghana

Holy Communion Set presented to Miracle Rock Church in Ghana
humbly Accepted by Rev. Dr. Charles Abban and his wife Lydia

The Holy Communion set was presented to Miracle Rock Church as a way of bridging together the Christian Church in America and Africa with the new covenant of peace and forgiveness of sins through the Holy Communion in honor of the sacrifice of Christ on the cross for all humanity.

The enslaved African descendants are joined by blood and lineage even if they are separated by geography forever. Thank you Barack and Michelle Obama for giving enslaved African descendants and the world hope. Earlier in this dissertation, I stated how happy I was to be an eyewitness at such a time in history as this to witness Senator Barack Obama as the first African American elected as the democratic candidate for President of the United States. With God, all things and goals are possible. It is an honor to complete this project as Barack Obama is elected as the first African American President of the United States.

Marlene and President Elect Barack Obama

The Enslaved African Ancestors have been Vindicated

The enslaved African ancestors can rest now! They have been vindicated by the election of Barack Obama, the child of an African father and an American mother. The African descendants have ascended from the Slave house to the White house, originally built by enslaved Africans. My prayer is that the world will see the hand of God working through President elect Obama to bring peace and harmony to the racially strained relationships between whites, blacks, browns, and all people around the world. Only time and attitudes will tell, but God's will, shall prevail. To God Be the Glory with the completion of this dissertation.

Endnotes:

(113) Breaking the Silence www.antislavery.org All Rights Reserved - Ghana.co.uk - 1999-2001

(114) Believe the Words and Inspirations of Desmond Tutu- Blue Mountain Press - 2007 (page 45)

(115) Mandela's Address at the Final Sitting of South Africa's First Democratically Elected Parliament March 1999

BIBLIOGRAPHY

Postma, Johannes Menne. *The Dutch in the Atlantic Slave Trade 1600-1815.* Cambridge University Press. 1990. New York, NY, USA. ISBN: 0521365856, pp.12.

Thomas, Hugh. *The History Of The Trans Atlantic Slave Trade 1440-1870.* Simon & Schuster Inc. New York, NY, USA ISBN: 0684835657, pp.1, 10, 11, 21-22, 24, 128.

Hennessy, James Pope. *The Atlantic Slave Traders 1441-1807.* Castle Books. 1967. Edison NJ. USA, ISBN: 0785815945, pp. 8 - 9, 12.

Felder, Cain Hope. *Holy Bible King James Version.* James C. Winston Publishing. 1993 Nashville, TN. USA, pp. 334, 1254.

Dr. King, Martin Luther Jr. *I Have A Dream.* Washington, D C. August 28, 1963

Adjai, Daniel. Ghanaian Tour Guide

Morganthau, Tom. *Slavery: How It Built the New World.* Newsweek Fall/Winter Special Issue. 1991. USA, pp. 66-69.

Brown, Beth Duff. *Ghana's Slave Castles Causing Controversy Five Centuries Later.* The Associated Press. ELMINA, Ghana. February 20, 1997.

History Today. Volume: 49 Issue: 8. August 1999. pp. 2-3

Adibe Patrick and Boateng Osei . New African March 2000 Issue, pp. 24, 26.

Gomez, Michael. *Reversing Sail A History of the African Diaspora.* Cambridge University Press. 2005 pp. 122, 126, 127.

Coffey, John. *The Abolition Of The Slave Trade: Christian Conscience And Political Action* Vol. 15, Number 2. June 2006

Klein, Herbert S. *The Atlantic Slave Trade*. New Approaches to the Americas. Cambridge University Press ISBN: 0521465885, pp.130

Segal, Ronald. *Islam's Black Slaves The other Black Diaspora.* Straus and Giroux, 2001.NewYork, NY Printed in the USA ISBN: 9780374227746, pp.1, 8, 9-10,

Bailey, Richard P. Rev. *from http://www.Answering Islam.org.* Vol. 4. 2004

Tamakloe, Winston and, Kodzobi, Adaklu. African Chiefs Must Apologise For Slave Trade. Ghanaian Times News 2007. pp. 16

Danquah Asirifi. *YAA ASANTEWAA* Books Limited Printed in KuMASI. Ashanti-Ghana. 2002 ISBN 9988-8028, pp. 2-3

Shinn, Florence Scovel. Simon & Schuster. 1925. New York, NY, ISBN 9743223470 pp.; 32-33

The Patriotic Vanguard - Sierre Leone Portal - Monday December 4 2006

African American Heritage Hymnal – GIA Publications, Inc. 2001 (Page 84)

Believe The Words and Inspirations of Desmond Tutu- Blue Mountain Press. 2007 pp. 22,45

Tamakloe, Winston and Kodzobi, Adaklu. *African Chiefs Must Apologise For Slave Trade*. Ghanaian Times News 2007. pp. 16

The Mariners' Museum 2002

Ghana Ministry of Tourism. *Joseph Project Souvenir Book.* 2007 pp. 3, 18. Christian Action Magazine. - South Africa – 2004

M'bokolo, Elikia. *The Impact Of The Slave Trade On Africa.* www. *Le Monde diplomatique* - April 2, 1998

Ghana.co.uk. *Breaking the Silence* www.antislavery.org All Rights Reserved - - 1999-2001

Hochschild, Adam. *King Leopold's Ghost: A Story of Greed, Terror, and Heroism in Colonial Africa.* Houghton Mifflin Books 1999

www.antislavery.com-BBC.co.uk- last updated January 22, 2007

The National Library of France, Paris

Bowen, Catherine Drinker *The Lion and the Throne*, a biography of Coke February 1552 3 September 1634 - April 1990

www.antislavery.com-BBC.co.uk - last updated January 22, 2007

Awake Watch Tower Bible and Tract Society. *Christianity and Slavery.* September 8, 2001

Abomey Historical Museum, Benin. www.epa-prema.net

Trollope. Fannie. *Domestic Manners of the Americans Dramatization* BBC February 1997

Rediker. Marcus. *The Slave Ship A Human History.* The Penquin Group. 2007 New York NY Printed in the USA pp. 16, 17-18, 19-20

Biko Steve. *No Fears Expressed Steve Biko.* Mutloatse Arts Heritage Trust. 2007 Printed in South Africa pp. 10

Mandela. Nelson. *Mandela's Address at the Final Sitting of South Africa's first Democratically Elected Parliament*, March 1999

Printed in the United States
220544BV00002B/1/P